THE LITTLE BOOK OF
MAHJONG
LEARN HOW TO PLAY, SCORE, AND WIN

SETH BROWN

ADAMS MEDIA
NEW YORK   LONDON   TORONTO   SYDNEY   NEW DELHI

Aadamsmedia

Adams Media
An Imprint of Simon & Schuster, Inc.
57 Littlefield Street
Avon, Massachusetts 02322

First Adams Media hardcover edition June 2018

ADAMS MEDIA and colophon are trademarks of Simon & Schuster.

For information about special discounts for bulk purchases, please contact Simon & Schuster Special Sales at 1-866-506-1949 or business@simonandschuster.com.

The Simon & Schuster Speakers Bureau can bring authors to your live event. For more information or to book an event contact the Simon & Schuster Speakers Bureau at 1-866-248-3049 or visit our website at www.simonspeakers.com.

Interior design by Colleen Cunningham
Interior images by Kathy Konkle; © 123RF/sahua
Technical review by Joan Mello

Manufactured in China

10 9 8 7 6 5 4 3 2 1

Library of Congress Cataloging-in-Publication Data
Brown, Seth, author.
The little book of mahjong / Seth Brown.
Avon, Massachusetts: Adams Media, 2018.
Series: The little book of.
Includes bibliographical references and index.
LCCN 2017057172 (print) | LCCN 2017058330 (ebook) | ISBN 9781507207390 (hc) | ISBN 9781507207406 (ebook)
LCSH: Mah jong. | BISAC: GAMES / Reference. | GAMES / Gambling / General. | GAMES / Board.
LCC GV1299.M3 (ebook) | LCC GV1299.M3 B76 2018 (print) | DDC 794--dc23
LC record available at https://lccn.loc.gov/2017057172

ISBN 978-1-5072-0739-0
ISBN 978-1-5072-0740-6 (ebook)

CONTENTS

Chapter 3. International Mahjong—

Chapter 4. International Mahjong—

Chapter 5. International Mahjong—

ACKNOWLEDGMENTS

My thanks go to:

- **Eileen from Simon & Schuster**—for reaching out and asking me to write this book
- **Debbie**—for encouragement and photos and everything else
- **Michelle**—for helping me maintain my sanity during the book-writing process
- **Jenn** and **Russ**—for hosting my favorite regular gaming night
- **Chris**—for lending me a fat-tile Mahjong set
- **Carol**—for looking at my American Mahjong notes and telling me about an updated rule
- **Other Mahjong experts**—whose work I could check to make sure I had my facts right (see the Bibliography and Resource List at the end of the book!)
- **My family**—for their constant support
- **Friendly gamers everywhere**—especially those who have played games with me or helped others learn more about games
- **Public libraries**—one of the last bastions of the public good; support your local library
- **Many more people**—but I hear the music and I think they're playing me off

INTRODUCTION

Thank you for picking up *The Little Book of Mahjong*. What follows is an easy and accessible introduction to Mahjong for players of all ages. It's never too late—or too early!—to start learning about the wonderful world of Mahjong.

This book is divided into four parts. The first part is a general overview of Mahjong, stretching from its origins in ancient China to the many variants of Mahjong played today. We'll discuss just how varied the different types of Mahjong are in Part 4, but the majority of this book focuses on the two most popular variants of Mahjong: International (Chinese) Mahjong, and American Mahjong. These two variants not only have different rules and scoring systems but even include different playing tiles!

Part 2 covers International Mahjong, the version of the game most commonly played at tournaments around the world. Based on the many regional variants played all over China, International Mahjong Rules involve trying to form sets called Chow, Pung, and Kong—otherwise known as three in a row, three of a kind, and four of a kind, respectively. When a player's hand is four such sets *and* a pair, that player may declare Mahjong (presuming their hand is worth at least 8 points—don't worry, we'll explain this later).

Part 3 focuses on American Mahjong, which has gained a lot of popularity in the United States, but has drifted far from the rules of its Chinese origins. American Mahjong adds eight Joker tiles, which count as wilds and can be used in any set of three (or more) of a kind. And you'll need them, because in American Rules you can only claim Mahjong by completing one of the specific hands indicated on a special scorecard, which changes annually. In addition, American Rules also add something called the Charleston, where players pass a few tiles to their opponents before starting play.

Don't worry if any of this sounds complicated. While scoring rules may seem overwhelming at first, keep in mind that Mahjong is just a game where your turn consists of simply drawing a tile and then discarding a tile. And what could be easier than that?

Whether you want to know more about Mahjong in general or are looking for a straightforward explanation of the rules, this book has you covered. Feel free to skip right to the strategy section for the International or American versions, or discover answers to your questions and ways to improve your game as you go.

PART 1

OVERVIEW OF MAHJONG

Before we leap right into the rules and strategy of Mahjong, it's worth taking a moment to talk about the game from a broader perspective. Why play it in the first place? When was it invented? How did a Chinese game become so popular in America? The answers to these questions and more—including Mahjong's Golden Rule—await you in the following pages.

CHAPTER 1

THE BASICS OF MAHJONG

Presumably, you wouldn't have picked up this book unless you already have some interest in Mahjong. And good for you! Mahjong is a fantastic game to learn, for a number of reasons. The game itself plays a little like Gin Rummy, insofar as it is a game involving drawing and discarding with the aim of getting a few sets in your hand. It's a game with enough skill to reward practiced players and smart play, but also involving enough luck that anyone can win. It's sufficiently complex to captivate players for a lifetime, yet is simple enough that you can learn it from this small book.

Mahjong is a game for all the senses. It has pieces that are inherently satisfying: the elegant look of the set, the tactile satisfaction of feeling the heft of the tiles, the sounds of mixing the pieces, the beauty of a built wall. And of course the pace of the game is generally active, since any player might declare Pung! or Call! and grab the tile you just discarded, even if it wasn't their turn. But for all the advantages of Mahjong as a game, its greatest advantage might be who plays it: everyone. Mahjong is rich with history and tradition, and has been played for generations by people all over the globe. It is a social game that builds community, as many get together with friends and family for a regular Mahjong game, often making an evening of it with food and copious conversation.

So whether you want a game of strategy or a game of luck, whether you like the pretty designs or the sound and feel of the pieces, whether your family has played for generations or you want to learn the game to play with some friends, no matter your age, gender, or heritage, Mahjong is the perfect game for you to learn.

The Origins of Mahjong

The origins of Mahjong are rich in variation and are not easily pinned to a clean and simple singular point of creation. Some have even claimed Noah played the game on the Ark, while other stories suggest that the game dates back to 1200 B.C. when the Bronze Age was giving way to the Iron Age and dominoes were common. A popular tale suggests that the great Chinese sage Confucius himself invented the game, citing the fact that the three dragons represent the Confucian virtues of benevolence, sincerity, and filial piety.

In reality, most experts believe that Mahjong evolved from similar games played in China within the last millennium. Games played by Chinese peasants in the 1100s and 1200s included "Kap Tai Shap," a game of Chinese dominoes, still enjoyed today, that uses a wall of tiles to draw from, as Mahjong does. The more relevant ancestor is a set of games such as "Luk Fu" that were played with "Money cards," a set of Chinese cards with suits that included "Coins," "Strings of Coins," and "Myriads" or "Wan," which were groupings of strings worth 10,000 coins. These correspond to the Coins, Strings, and Wan on today's Mahjong tiles.

Mahjong has many names. Not only in Chinese—where it has gone by Mahjong, Mah Jongg, Ma Chong, Ma Jiang, Ma Cheuk, Pe-Ling, Pung-Chow, and Ma Que—but also in English, where it is known by many nicknames, including "The Game of Sparrows" (as translated from *Ma Que*), "Clattering Sparrows" (a reference to the sound of the tiles being swirled on the table), "Flax Commander" (as translated from *Mah Jongg*), "Game of a Hundred Intelligences" (named for the strategy required), or "Game of a Thousand Wonders" (named for the dynamic nature of play).

Yet perhaps the most promising lineage to Mahjong can be traced back to a set of card games starting with Yeh Tzu—which became Ye

Zi Jiu Pai, and eventually just Ya Pei—which involved a deck of oblong cards that included four Flowers, just as modern Mahjong does. It was Ya Pei that eventually evolved into the game that most scholars agree was the direct ancestor of Mahjong: Matiao.

Matiao or Ma Diao ("Hanging Horse"), also known as Yezi ("Leaf"), was popular in the Ming Dynasty from the fifteenth to seventeenth centuries, and used the money card decks of the other games previously mentioned, featuring the Coins, Strings, and Wan that would eventually form the basic suits of Mahjong. Matiao was played on paper cards, and so scholars believe that it was the merging of the card games like Matiao with the tiles used in other games that created Mahjong.

Matiao was not the only card game with similarities to Mahjong. Games like Kan Hu had not only the three money suits of Coins, Strings, and Wan, but also the Redflower, Whiteflower, and Old Thousand (analog to the three Dragons of Mahjong), and players could even declare "Pung" to claim another player's discarded card to complete a set of three.

The Creation of Mahjong

Sadly, no records exist to tell the exact mix of prior games that went into Mahjong's creation. But we do have a date for the origination of the game in 1850. And there are a few theories as to the game's creator: some attribute it to Hung Siu Chen, the leader of the Taiping Rebellion. Others believe it was an unnamed Chinese nobleman in Shanghai, or unnamed Chinese army officers. Still others believe it was conceived by a pair of brothers in the city of Ningpo.

But the preponderance of evidence points to one man as the father of Mahjong: Chen Yumen of Ningpo. Like Mahjong itself, Chen Yumen was known by a few different names, including Chen Yu-mun, Chin Zheng Yue, Yanglou, Zhengyue, and Zhengyao. Yumen is said to have turned the paper cards of Matiao into tiles to make the game more elegant, and he is also credited with adding the Wind tiles to the four copies of numbers in three Coin-based suits.

> Chen Yumen was also an army officer during the Taiping Rebellion, and living in a culture where credit was often given to one's superiors to bestow greater glory upon them, this might well account for the theory that it was the leader of the Rebellion that invented Mahjong; Chen Yumen may well have given the credit to his leader!

With tiles made of ivory and bamboo, Mahjong sets were not cheap to acquire, making it a game for the aristocracy—especially because the government at the time only allowed the mandarin aristocrats at the emperor's court to play, lest the peasants learn the rules and become so smart that they rebel. Thus, for over half a century, Mahjong remained a game only for elites.

The year 1911 marked the fall of the Manchu Dynasty and the election of the first president of the Republic of China, Sun Yat-sen. A democratizing wave of reforms swept the country in many respects as the ruling class fell. Many of these social changes had radical effects on the populace, but most important for our purposes is that Mahjong was now available for every commoner in the country to enjoy. It became known as "the people's game" as all classes learned it, swiftly making it the most popular game in the country.

Mahjong Meets the World

As Mahjong became available for all of China to enjoy, its popularity soared. Mahjong was being played in every province, and even if each location had its own variants of rules for the game (and often their own names for the game), the fact remained that Mahjong mania was sweeping the country. But it certainly wouldn't stop there. By the 1920s, people from all over the globe who had spent time in China would bring the game back to their respective home countries, immediately igniting interest.

America

An oilman named Joseph Park Babcock had been working as the Soochow city representative for the Standard Oil Company, living in Shanghai. During his time in Shanghai, he saw the growing popularity of Mahjong, and even played it in the local English clubs. It was there that Babcock and his friends began putting small Arabic numerals in the upper corners of the tiles, making them easier for Americans to read, especially the Wan (Characters) suit.

In 1920, Babcock brought the first sets of Mah-Jongg (having trademarked the transliteration in that spelling) to the United States. In order to avoid the difficulty of the myriad regional differences of gameplay rules across China (and to ease Americans into a strange, foreign game), Babcock wrote a manual of simplified rules titled *Babcock's Rules for Mah-Jongg: The Red Book of Rules*. He packaged this manual with all the sets he was selling.

In 1923, Babcock returned to America and patented the name Mah-Jongg internationally. In the roaring 1920s, it was popular to play with fancy hand-carved sets of ivory and bamboo. Two years later, lumber merchant W.A. Hammond helped Babcock import less-expensive Chinese-made sets of bone. This turned out to be a big tipping point in bringing the game to more Americans, increasing the value of Mahjong imports nearly thirty-fold over the previous year.

The demand in America exploded, to the point where the United States was shipping vast quantities of cattle shinbones to China, so they could craft more bone Mahjong tiles to ship back to the US. Seeing the huge import market, American companies leaped into Mahjong with both feet. Parker Brothers signed a deal with Babcock to be able to use his trademarked "Mah-Jongg" name, and would include his book of instructions and rules in all their Mahjong sets, which they produced in a variety of materials and prices ranging from elegant ivory to cheap wood.

Parker Brothers was thwarted by other companies eager to cash in on the craze, avoiding trademark or patent infringement by naming their games something different (like "Pung Chow") and including slightly different rules than Babcock's. Some records argue that Milton Bradley was saved from bankruptcy by a huge demand for cheap Mahjong sets.

Mahjong quickly took over the country, from players who would have Mahjong nights at their homes, to the Mahjong parlors that began to pop up across the nation. Mahjong appeared on the cover of *The Saturday Evening Post*, and was even covered in a popular (and unfortunately racist) song by Eddie Cantor: "Since Ma Is Playing Mah Jong." Soon, Mahjong had become so popular that the simplified rules Babcock created were no longer holding people's attention. Players began inventing their own rules and adding new special hands. Regional rules proliferated, but without standard gameplay, American enthusiasm for Mahjong began to wane.

Japan

Japan had technically been introduced to Mahjong over the prior decade, when teacher Hikosaku Nakawa brought home some sets from China, and when Shou Kan Seki had written up a detailed Japanese description of Mahjong rules in Shanghai. But if one man was responsible for bringing Mahjong to Japan in a big way, it was a soldier named Saburo Hirayama.

Hirayama started a Mahjong school and Mahjong parlor called the Nan-nan Club in 1924, and the game quickly became popular. Later that very year, the first nationwide tournament was held. This was a great testament to the speed at which Mahjong had gained favor in Japan, but as a tournament, it was somewhat of a failure. One of the main issues was that, like in China, people from all over Japan were playing with slightly different variants and rules, making a standardized tournament difficult to adjudicate.

This led directly to the formation of the Kansai Mah-Jongg Federation, which created a unified rule set known as the Japan Mah-Jongg Standard Rules. Though this was a simplified rule set when compared with the Chinese version of the game, the standardization of rules helped further bolster its popularity. Mahjong became so popular that Japanese people were still playing it decades later despite a government ban on Mahjong (instated due to the war with China). In the 1960s a slightly more complicated version of Japanese Mahjong was created, called Riichi (Reach) Mahjong, and this is the variant most popular today.

Mahjong in Europe

In 1923, a Dutch news magazine published a letter to the editor from one "J.P." of Amsterdam, who had written to inquire if anyone was familiar with the Chinese game of Mah-Jongg. He described the game of ivory or bone tiles with Chinese symbols, looking vaguely like dominoes, and was eager to know if the game had yet reached Holland. The editor of the news magazine asked his readers if anyone knew where the game was available. This inquiry prompted Perry & Co. of Amsterdam to talk with their international branches, including a Dutch division in America that had seen Babcock's success with Mahjong, and so Perry & Co. quickly began selling Mahjong sets in Holland. It wasn't long before a Netherlands Mah-Jongg League was founded.

Meanwhile in France at around the same time, the French were undergoing their own version of Mahjong fever. Their reaction to the game was uniquely French; they were not actually overly excited about the game of Mahjong itself, but were mesmerized by the artistry of Mahjong sets. Many elaborately detailed Mahjong sets were purchased as objects for display, even if they were rarely used to play. France was even enamored of the trappings and designs of Mahjong, seeing sales of Mahjong-themed accessories.

The United Kingdom

England's introduction to the game also happened in 1921. L.L. Harr was an Englishman who befriended the Chinese statesman Li Hung Chang, who taught Harr a version of Mahjong called Pe-Ling. Harr brought a few sets of the game to England, which caught on so swiftly that before Harr had even disembarked from his ship voyage back to England he had already made Pe-Ling fans of a number of his fellow English passengers. The Pe-Ling version of Mahjong was only more popular once Harr had landed, catching on quickly with the nobility of London. Mahjong clubs sprang up all over England.

America Standardizes the Rules

Back in the United States, arguments over rules were intensifying. In addition to the usual regional variances that one expects with any game spread from friend to friend (because all of the companies producing Mahjong sets wanted to avoid trademark infringement), many enthusiasts were inventing their own sets of rules. Babcock wanted to settle the matter once and for all. In 1924, Babcock gathered the authors of the main competing Mahjong rule sets of the time and formed the Standardization Committee of the American Official Laws of Mah-Jongg. The members were Joseph P. Babcock, Robert F. Foster, Lee F. Hartman, John H. Smith, and Milton C. Work.

This group worked together to create *The American Code of Laws for Mah-Jongg*, which codified official rules to bridge the gap between the many variants played across the country, summarized the traditional Chinese rules, and added a new American way to play. This slowed the chaos of divergent variants across the country, but did not stop it, as players continued to add their own combinations of special hands and ignore others.

The persistence of American Mahjong today can probably be credited to the National Mah Jongg League (NMJL), which was formed in New York in 1937 by Viola Cecil, Dorothy Meyerson, Herma Jacobs, and Hortense Potter. Cecil, the president of the group, called the new American Mahjong "Maajh" in her book *Maajh: The American Version of an Ancient Chinese Game*. Like Babcock before them, the NMJL standardized the rules and the scoring hands to make sure that American Mahjong players around the country were abiding by the same rules. But the biggest innovation of the NMJL was to solve the problem that had plagued Babcock and those before him: Mahjong players eventually grew bored with the game and wanted to add their own special hands.

NMJL's solution? An ever-changing scorecard detailing the scoring hands, which was updated annually by the League to have a new and different list of special hands. This had two great advantages for maintaining and fomenting interest in Mahjong. First, players never had a chance to get bored with the special hands of the game, because they would be changed every year. This prevented much of the new hands and variations that had thwarted earlier efforts at standardization.

Just as important, however, was the fact that players would now need to contact the NMJL each year to receive the newly updated scorecard. And as you might expect, players regularly in contact with the regulating body of American Mahjong looking to buy scoring cards ended up also purchasing other Mahjong accoutrements, asking for rule clarifications, or learning about and attending League-sanctioned events.

The combination of these two factors had led the NMJL to persist for over three-quarters of a century in New York, with a membership that has grown from its initial thirty-two members to over a third of a million today.

China Makes It Legal

By the 1920s Mahjong had finally become available for everyone in the country, and each province was putting their own spin on the game. The popularity continued until 1967, when Chairman Mao Zedong's Cultural Revolution cracked down on gambling. Mahjong was considered part of the old ways, and, as a gambling game, was an evil element of corruption to be destroyed. Ironically, the banning of Mahjong in China led to it becoming even more popular in nearby places like Hong Kong, Taiwan, Vietnam, Korea, and more.

In the 1980s, after Mao's death, Mahjong had a resurgence in China, only without the gambling element. But this only lasted a few years, until the game's history in gambling parlors reasserted itself, and people were once again playing for money. In 1998, in an attempt to keep gambling out of Mahjong and to standardize the rules, the State Sports Commission of China recognized Mahjong as a national sport. They also sanctioned the Official International Rules, a result of two years of work by experts and researchers across China, who boiled down 440 hands to 200 and then to the 81 that are used around the world today, and which are detailed in Part 2 of this book.

The Different Types of Mahjong

Now that you know a bit about the background of Mahjong, it's time to learn how to play! Two paths lie before you: International Mahjong or American Mahjong. International Mahjong, covered in Part 2, is played in competitions around the globe, and is also similar to most of the myriad variants that exist around the world. For this reason, if you know nothing about Mahjong, this is a sensible place to start. (It's also why it comes next in the book!) International Mahjong is played pretty much everywhere, making it a variant that is certainly worth learning. Compared with American Mahjong, International Mahjong is a lot more open with what constitutes a winning hand. You have some leeway to assemble a hand in your own way, and many people enjoy the challenge. The only real downside of International Mahjong is that the 81 scoring fans (a collection of sets in a hand worth a certain number of points) take some getting used to. There are a lot of them, and while you can memorize the scoring fans with enough play, you'll definitely find them too much to keep in mind for your first few plays. But there's nothing wrong with having this book on hand to look things up, with a bookmark in the scoring section (Chapter 4).

If that's too much at the moment, you can also start with the Primary Scoring Rules listed immediately after the Regular Scoring Rules. Using only half the amount of scoring fans, the simplified version is designed to help people ease into the International Mahjong Scoring system. And if that's still too much for your first game, don't worry! Just try the "Simple/Casual" variant at the beginning of Chapter 4—this eliminates all of the scoring rules entirely (and admittedly, a lot of the strategy), and will let you focus on just learning the basic mechanics of the game.

American Mahjong, which will be covered in Part 3, is a very different game. It is rarely played outside of the United States, and plays very differently from most other Mahjong variants. It is, however, the Mahjong variant of choice for many segments of this country. The National Mah Jongg League (NMJL) has a vibrant membership and sells annual scorecards to most regular players of American Mahjong.

These scorecards are required to play the game in most circles, as the only legal winning hands are those listed on the scorecards, and these change from year to year. The good news is that all players play with the cards directly in front of them, so it is easy for a new player to refer to the card during play. Because the hands are strictly limited to the specific combinations on the card, there is less free reign in assembling your hand. The addition of the Charleston (more on this in Chapter 8) adds another interesting element to the game, allowing players to pass tiles to improve their hand before the game even starts. American Mahjong also tends to use racks to hold tiles (these are not a necessity) and has eight extra Joker tiles.

If you have any friends who play American Mahjong, or live in a community of people who play it, you'll likely want to skip ahead to Part 3 and start by learning it first. But otherwise we'd encourage you to learn the two games in the order presented, if only so you can encounter International Rules as "This is a standard Mahjong variant" and the American Rules as "This is a special and uniquely American variant."

Playing by the Table Rules

The Golden Rule of Mahjong is this:

The table makes the rules.

What does that mean? It means that if you are a new player joining a preexisting Mahjong table, then you should expect to play by whatever variants being used. You may think that by learning American Mahjong, that if your table also plays American Mahjong, you are inherently playing the same variant. Well, yes and no. You are playing the same overarching variant, which is American Mahjong. But many players play with a variety of house rules that can change the game quite a bit. Your table may play with any number of unofficial rules and variations, including:

- Using extra Jokers.
- Picking the seating, dealer, and wall break differently.
- Setting aside a Dead Wall.
- Agreeing on the third pass of the Charleston.
- Using different ways to announce discarded Jokers.
- Prioritizing discards by first-to-call, rather than by next player.
- Picking Ahead (a.k.a. "fourteen-tile" Mahjong), where players all draw their next tile before their turn.

The International Rules system is not immune to discrepancies, and can have house rules for things like allowing Mixed hands (Pungs and/or Chows that contain one number from each suit, rather than mandating all from one suit) and any number of scoring differences deviating from the official rules.

Whenever you are a newcomer to a table, even if you know which rule system is being employed, it is worth asking for a rundown of any play variants, lest you be caught off guard by a rule. When you join a table, the rules should be explained to you (if not in full, at least as they differ from the official rules), and you should then follow the rules of the table.

Note that rules can and will differ very much from table to table! Picking Ahead is a standard variant that many groups demand, because they want everyone to be planning a strategy before their turn. However, it is also a variant that in many other groups will result in you being disqualified from the game for having the wrong number of tiles in your hand.

Likewise, some tables play a very fast and unforgiving game, where players only have a second or two to claim the discard before the next player racks a tile. Other tables take a more leisurely approach and give everyone plenty of time. Attempting to use the rules of one table at the other will end poorly. Respect the fact that each group may have developed its own variants over time, and understand that you will usually have to play in the manner the other players prefer.

All of the aforementioned advice, of course, is only for preexisting tables. If there is no history of playing Mahjong together among the players at your table, simply discuss and agree what rules to use. It is strongly recommended that you use no variants at first. There will be plenty of variants later, but you may as well play by the official rules to begin with.

And even if you are joining a preexisting table, you can certainly ask them if they wouldn't mind playing at a more leisurely pace and with fewer variants—many tables will oblige while you learn the game. Just remember that if they want to play with a certain variant, that is their right.

PART 2

INTERNATIONAL MAHJONG

International Mahjong, also known as Mahjong Competition Rules or Official Mahjong, is the most recognized Mahjong variant in the world. As you may recall from Chapter 1, China recognized Mahjong as a national sport in 1998, and assembled experts from around the country to help blend the nation's many variants into a single set of rules. This newly codified International Rules system became the standard for tournaments in China and around the globe. In this part, you'll learn how to play this popular variant, as well as a few good strategies for beginners.

CHAPTER 2

INTERNATIONAL MAHJONG— TILE GUIDE

This chapter will explore the various types of tiles used in the standard International Mahjong game. You'll learn what the tiles look like, some of the symbolism behind them, and easy ways to remember which tile is which.

Suits

The standard International Mahjong set uses 144 tiles, which break down into three suits. There are four copies each of 1 through 9 in the three suits, making thirty-six tiles of each suit.

Dots

Dots are sometimes called Circles, Targets, Balls, Coins (representing the old Chinese coins with holes in the middle), or Wheels (representing the wheel of heaven), but are usually simply called Dots. They are the easiest suit to understand, because simply counting the number of dots will tell you what number tile you have. One big dot for the 1, two dots for the 2, and so on.

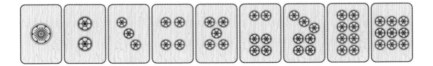

Bamboo

Bamboo tiles are occasionally known as Sticks, Spears, Boos, or even Strings (so named for being shaped like the strings of old Chinese coins), but are generally called Bam when discussing the game, and represent the axis of Earth. Like with the Dots, the number of bamboos on a tile directly corresponds to its number. The only tricky thing is the Bam1, which instead of a single bamboo stick has a picture of a bird. Don't confuse the bird for a bonus tile; it's just a 1 of Bamboo, and can be used in Chows and Pungs accordingly.

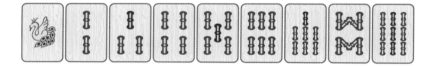

Characters

Characters are the Chinese characters for the numbers 1 through 9, all written over the Chinese symbol for 10,000, known as Wan. These vaguely follow the coin theme by representing 10,000 coins, and follow the heaven and Earth theme by representing the life of man, but most everyone simply refers to them as Crak, as shorthand for *Character*.

If you do not read Chinese (and do not have an American Mahjong set with Arabic numerals on them), you may find it difficult to remember which character corresponds to which number at first. But don't panic!

Here are some easy mental tricks to remember which symbol is which number.

- The 1, 2, and 3 are made of one, two, and three horizontal lines.
- The 4 is a rectangle with four sides.
- The 5 looks a little like a guy on a surfboard who would totally give you a high five. (Five is the most difficult one to remember, so you can always just place it by process of elimination.)
- The 6 looks a little like a stick figure, so remember that stick figure means 6 figure.
- The 7 looks like an upside-down 7 with a dash in the middle.
- The 8 looks like an upside-down V, which you can remember by drinking your V-8.
- The 9 looks like a lowercase n, so remember that n is for 9.

Honors

In addition to the three main suits, there are also two types of Honors tiles: Winds and Dragons. Note that Honors tiles have no numbers associated with them.

Winds

There are four copies each of the four Winds: North, South, East, and West. The Winds are of high importance in International Mahjong, with a Prevailing Wind for the round, as well as each player being assigned a Wind at each match, with the East Wind always dealing.

In Chinese tradition, these are ordered East, South, West, North. Some Mahjong sets have a small English letter in the corner to indicate the Wind direction. If yours do not, the symbols can be difficult to remember, but you can try to make out the first capital letter of each Wind direction in its figure—the horizontal lines of the E on the top of East, a big diagonal S spanning the whole South tile, a W on the bottom of the West tile, and the entire North tile looking like a backward N.

Dragons

There are also four copies each of the three Dragons.

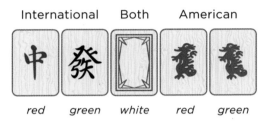

The Red and Green Dragons are sometimes Chinese characters and sometimes just pictures of dragons, but are always easily identified because they are actually red and green. The Red Dragon Chun symbolizes the middle order of man, and hence is connected with the Crak suit thematically. The Green Dragon Fa symbolizes plant life on Earth, and thus connects with the Bams.

The White Dragon Po or Bai represents heaven, and thus is connected with the Dots suit. While occasionally dragon-shaped, Po is traditionally represented by a rectangular shape, which is why it is often referred to as a "Soap," because of its resemblance to a soap bar. A blank tile (that also looks like a bar of soap) is sometimes used to represent the White Dragon, who, being the same white color as the background of the tile, cannot be seen.

Bonus Tiles (Flowers and Seasons)

The Flowers and Seasons tiles, which are not used to make hands, are placed to the side when drawn and are worth points when scoring. While there are four copies of all the other tiles mentioned previously, there is only a single copy of each of the eight bonus tiles.

Each of the Flowers and Seasons is associated with a particular Wind, in numerical order of the Winds as noted previously.

- 1 (Plum Flower, Spring Season) connects to the East Wind
- 2 (Lily, Summer) is the South Wind
- 3 (Chrysanthemum, Autumn) is the West Wind
- 4 (Bamboo Flower, Winter) is the North Wind; do not confuse the Bamboo Flower bonus tile with the suit of Bams 1 through 9—it is not related

In many variations players may score bonus points for playing a Flower that matches either the Prevailing Wind or their own seat. But in standard International Competition Rules, all Flowers and Seasons are treated equally: they are immediately set aside when drawn to serve as a bonus point at the end of game, and then replaced with another draw.

Non-Tile Components

In addition to the tiles, you will also find some other pieces in your Mahjong set. There is also a pair of standard six-sided dice, rolled to determine the break point. Some sets also include a dealer marker (to sit in front of the dealer so players recall who is East), which sometimes includes a Prevailing Wind marker (to track the round).

Racks (and pushers) tend not to be used in International Mahjong, as the tiles are generally thick enough to stand on their own. Many players use chips or scoring sticks instead of money, in which case each player must start with an equal value of chips. This can range from 500 to 20,000 depending on the table.

CHAPTER 3

INTERNATIONAL MAHJONG – SETUP AND GAMEPLAY

Now that you are familiar with the tiles used to play International Mahjong, we can discuss the setup and play of the game. While some of the traditional setup procedures may seem a little confusing at first, rest assured that once you get started you'll find the gameplay very straightforward and easy to understand.

Seating the Dealer

Before you can start the game, the first thing you must do is select a dealer. In modern International Rules, this is done by taking one copy of each of the four Winds (East, South, West, North), shuffling them all facedown, and having each player draw one. The players then re-seat themselves counterclockwise in the following order: East, South, West, North.

If you don't want to get up, you can skip the initial seating reassignments by shuffling the four Wind tiles as previously mentioned but simply declaring whoever draws East as East, and then ignoring the other three Wind tiles drawn to assign the rest of the Winds counterclockwise to players as they are already sitting (East, South, West, North).

Rounds and Prevailing Winds

In the International Rules, a game of Mahjong consists of sixteen hands, divided into four rounds in which each player deals once. The Prevailing

Wind starts at East along with the dealer, and moves from East to South to West to North. Within each Prevailing Wind round, the deal will move from East to South to West to North.

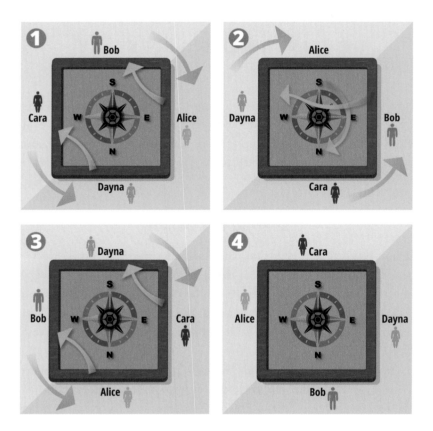

Official International Rules involve a somewhat complex seating shuffle. After the four hands of the East Prevailing Wind round, the North and West players swap seats, and the East and South players swap seats, so the former South player is now East for the next round (hence "South Prevailing Wind"). The third round is the most confusing: North (formerly West) moves right one seat to become East, while

West (formerly North) moves left one seat to become South. Meanwhile South (formerly East) crosses the table to become North, and East crosses the table to become West. For the final round, South and East swap seats, and North and West swap seats.

This complex dance assures not only that each player gets a chance to deal as East to start a round but also that the players will get a chance to sit on the left of each other player, eliminating any advantage of someone going after a particular player. If this play of musical chairs seems too complicated, feel free to just say that South Prevailing Wind means that South has the first deal of the second round, and don't bother getting up. Every Mahjong table has its own rules, after all. Either way, the most important thing to know is that the East Wind is always the dealer.

Creating the Wall

All 144 tiles are placed facedown in the middle of the table, and then all the players help mix the pieces up thoroughly with both hands. This is sometimes known as "washing the tiles," and may continue for longer than you expect, but it is an important part of the traditional Mahjong setup ritual. This process is often very loud, as the tiles need to be thoroughly mixed, and the sounds they make as they clack and clatter against one another may be the reason for the name *Mahjong* (Chinese for "Sparrow Tiles" or "Game of Sparrows"). For this reason, the shuffling of the tiles is often referred to as the "twittering of sparrows" or "clattering of sparrows"—so try to enjoy the noise!

As the tiles are being mixed, try to keep them facedown as much as possible. If some tiles end up getting flipped face-up (which is very likely), simply flip them facedown and continue mixing. Once the tiles are all thoroughly mixed, each player takes facedown tiles and builds a wall in front of themselves. The wall should be two tiles high, and eighteen tiles long. Players using a Mahjong table with a lip edge will often square their lines of tiles against it.

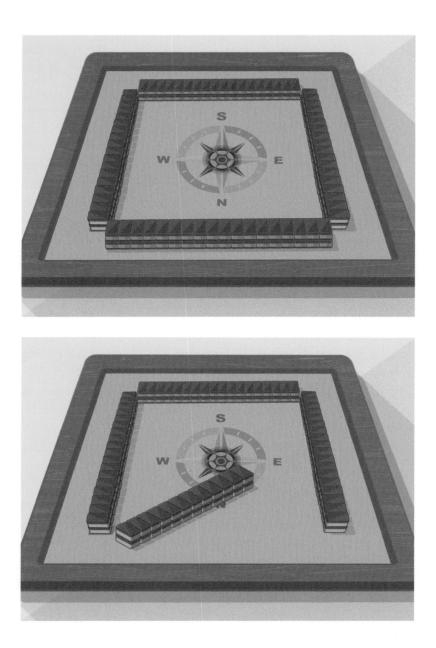

PART 2. INTERNATIONAL MAHJONG

Once all players have built their walls, the four walls are pushed toward the center of the table, making them easier for all players to reach. This generally forms a square, although some players prefer to tilt the walls slightly diagonally so the edges of the square stick out.

Distributing the Tiles

The dealer (East) rolls two dice to determine the break point in the wall. (Some variants use three dice instead.) The break point is the point where the tiles are separated and dealt from. First, the dice are thrown to determine who has the starting wall. The dealer counts counterclockwise, with the dealer's own wall (East) counting as 1, South as 2, West as 3, North as 4, East again as 5, and so on until the appropriate number is reached (e.g., if the dice roll a 7—a frequent occurrence!—West will be the starting wall).

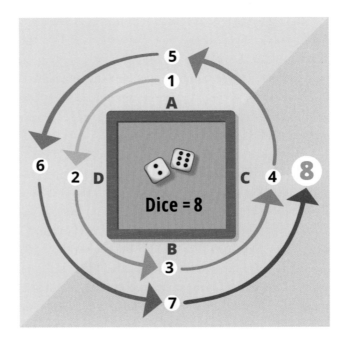

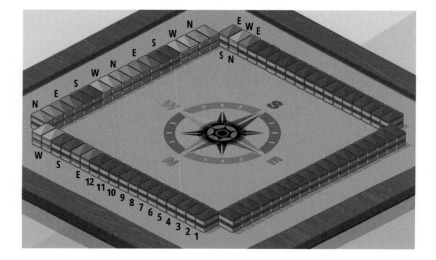

Once a starting wall has been chosen, it is time to choose a break point. The dealer throws the dice a second time. (Some variants have the starting wall owner throw the dice for their second roll, or even skip the second roll entirely and just use the number rolled initially to choose the starting wall.) However the second number is determined, the player on the starting wall counts that many tiles from the right edge of his wall, and separates the wall at that point to make a break.

With a break in the wall now accomplished, East then takes the first two stacks (four tiles) from the left of the break point. South takes the next four tiles, West the next four, and North the next four. This is repeated twice more around the table, so each player has twelve tiles.

The final tiles are taken in one of two ways. Traditionally, East takes one more stack of tiles (two tiles), South then takes the next top tile, West takes the revealed bottom tile, and North takes a final top tile.

However, in the Chan-Chan variation, East takes the first and third available top tiles, leaving a pattern that looks a bit like a crenellated castle wall. South then takes the first revealed bottom tile, West takes the next top tile, and North takes the next (newly revealed) bottom tile. When East takes the two nonconsecutive tiles, they often click together, and it is this sound that gives the Chan-Chan variation its name.

Replacements

Finally, the dealer has fourteen tiles, and all other players have thirteen tiles. You are almost ready to begin the game! The final step is to deal with the bonus tiles: Flowers and Seasons. If you have any of these in your hand, reveal them immediately by placing them face-up in front of you, and (in turn order, starting with East) draw a replacement tile from the back end of the wall.

While bonus tiles are being replaced, players may also declare a Concealed Kong (four of the same tile) by melding the Kong facedown in front of them and drawing one replacement tile from the back end of the wall. Because a Mahjong requires four sets and a pair, Kongs use an extra tile as compared to a Chow (a run of three consecutive tiles in the same suit) or Pung (three of a kind of an identical tile), which is why whenever a player decides to form a Kong they must draw a single replacement tile in order to be able to make the correct number of sets. Also, note that a Kong is the only concealed set that is ever melded to the table. It remains facedown because it is concealed, but must be placed on the table in order to be declared and to justify the drawing of a replacement tile. (And don't try to cheat, because all Concealed Kongs are revealed at the end of a game!) Once all bonus tiles (and optionally, Concealed Kongs) have been replaced, you are now ready to start the game, by having the dealer discard a tile.

Starting the Round

With the players seated, the wall built, and opening hands taken, it's finally time to start the game. Your goal in the game is to create a "Mahjong," which is a hand of four groups and one pair. In order to claim

Mahjong, your hand must also be worth at least 8 points, which will be covered in detail in the scoring chapter (Chapter 4). But for now, just keep in mind that your goal is to have four groups and a pair.

It is technically possible that the East player will start the hand by being dealt a complete Mahjong. (This is incredibly rare, but in the unlikely event it happens, East simply reveals their hand and claims Mahjong.) Chances are, you will never see this happen, in which case East starts the hand by discarding a tile. Whenever a tile is discarded, all players have a few seconds to claim it before the next player starts their turn. If no one does, the turn passes counterclockwise around the table, which means that after East it is the South player (on East's right) that goes next.

On Your Turn

When it is your turn to play, you should:

1. **Wait.** Allow a few seconds to see if anyone (possibly you!) wants to claim the most recently discarded tile. If so, skip the rest of this section and move to the following "Claiming the Discard" section.
2. **Draw the next tile from the wall.** The next tile will always be clockwise from the break point. If there is a single bottom tile with nothing stacked atop it, that's the next tile. If not, take the top tile from the next stack.
3. **Bonus tiles!** If your newly drawn tile is one of the eight bonus tiles (Flowers or Seasons), immediately play it face-up to the upper corner of your play area, and draw a replacement from the back of the wall (the first tile going counterclockwise from the break point). This will be worth a bonus point if you achieve Mahjong. If your replacement tile is another bonus tile, repeat this process; otherwise, proceed to Step 4.
4. **Is it Mahjong?** See if your hand now contains a valid Mahjong, meaning four sets and a pair. If not, proceed to Step 5. If you do

have four sets and a pair, keep in mind that under International Rules you must have 8 points in order to claim your Mahjong. (If you are playing with simple scoring, there is no point minimum to declare Mahjong—skip ahead to "Declaring Mahjong.") Under International Rules, some circumstances will automatically qualify you to claim Mahjong (such as forming a Mahjong with the replacement tile you draw for forming a Kong, or with the last tile in the game), but most of the time you'll need to add up the values of your hand, which will be covered in Chapter 4.

If you add up the point values and have at least 8 points, you can declare Mahjong and win the round! Skip ahead to the "Declaring Mahjong" section. Otherwise, even if you have four sets and a pair, you can't declare Mahjong with fewer than 8 points under International Scoring, so move on to Step 5.

5. **Kong check!** Check to see if the tile you just drew completes a Kong (four of a kind). If so, you may choose to play it. There are two types of Kongs you might make by drawing a tile from the wall:

- Melded Kong—If you already have a Melded Pung (three of a kind) revealed on the table, and you draw the fourth identical tile off the wall, you may play it face-up to improve your Pung into a Kong. Every Melded Kong is worth 1 point when you declare Mahjong.

- Concealed Kong—If the drawn tile gives you four of a kind in your hand, you may place all four of them *facedown* on the table as a Concealed Kong. This will not only hide the identity of the tiles from your opponents, but a Concealed Kong is additionally worth 2 points when you declare Mahjong.

(Keep in mind that just because you *can* play a Kong doesn't mean that you necessarily should. For example, imagine that you are holding Bam3, Bam3, Bam3, Bam4, Bam5, and you draw a Bam3 off the wall. You might decide to meld a Concealed Kong of Bam3s. But you might also decide that your hand would be better off with a Pung of three Bams, and a Chow of Bam3, Bam4, Bam5. This strategy will be discussed in Chapter 5, but for now, just remember that declaring a Kong from your hand is always optional.)

Either way, if you decide to declare a Kong, after placing your Kong on the table you immediately draw a replacement tile from the back end of the wall. (Note: if you have drawn the last tile from the wall, and there are no replacement tiles, you are not allowed to declare a Kong.)

Theoretically, it is possible that this new tile might complete another Kong for you, in which case you can repeat this entire step. Or it might be another bonus tile, in which case you can repeat Step 3. Otherwise, presuming you still can't declare Mahjong, proceed to Step 6.

6. **Discard a tile.** Pick a tile from your hand that you no longer want, and place it face-up in the middle of the table. (Some variants have each player arrange their discards in front of themselves, but this is less common for casual games.) Once you have discarded a tile, your turn is over. The turn will then pass counterclockwise to the next player, unless someone claims the discard.

Claiming the Discard

Whenever a tile is discarded, before the next player starts their turn, there is a short window of a few seconds when any player may claim the most recently discarded tile. If playing with any new players, it is recommended that this window of opportunity last a little longer. Experienced players will likely shorten this window.

A player may claim the most recently discarded tile by declaring the reason for which they are claiming the tile. If multiple players claim a tile, here are the priorities in descending order:

1. **Mahjong.** Any player may declare Mahjong and claim the most recently discarded tile to form a Mahjong, whether it completes a

Pung, a Chow, or even a pair. A player claiming a tile to make a Mahjong has priority over all other claims. If multiple players claim the same tile for Mahjong, priority goes to the player whose turn was coming soonest, e.g., highest priority to the right of the discarding player. (Some variants assign priority based on the value of the set being completed, or even allow multiple winners.) In the case of a tile being claimed for Mahjong, the round is ended, and the claiming player is the winner. Skip the rest of this section and see the next section under "Declaring Mahjong" for more information.

2. **Pung and Kong.** If no player is claiming the most recently discarded tile for Mahjong, any player may claim a tile for a Pung (three identical tiles) or Kong (four identical tiles) by declaring Pung or Kong.

- For a Pung, the claiming player takes the discarded tile, places it with two matching tiles from her hand, and lays all three face-up in front of her as a set. This is considered a Melded Pung. (In some variants, the left, right, or center tile of the Pung is placed on its side to indicate which other player discarded the third tile.) The melding player then discards a tile as if it were the end of her turn, and play continues to her right.

- For a Kong, the claiming player matches the discard with three tiles from her hand instead of two, thereby creating a set of four identical tiles. As always when melding a Kong, the claiming player then immediately draws a replacement tile from the back of the wall, before discarding a tile to end her turn and have play proceed to her right.

- Note: a discard may *not* be claimed to expand a Melded Pung into a Kong. The only way you may upgrade a Revealed Pung into a Kong is by drawing the tile you need directly from the wall, or already having it in your hand. Discards may only be used to form a Melded Kong if you have a Concealed Pung in your hand.

3. **Chow.** If no player is claiming the most recently discarded tile for Mahjong, and it is not superseded by a player claiming Pung or Kong,

then the player directly to the right of the discarding player may declare Chow in order to claim the tile for use in a Chow (three consecutive tiles in the same suit). Note that this option is *only* available to the player whose turn would naturally be next, and while claiming a discard for Mahjong, Pung, or Kong can allow players to take a turn out of order, calling for a Chow merely continues the flow of play.

- For claiming a Chow: the calling player picks up the discarded tile, along with two other tiles of the same suit from his hand, and lays down a face-up run of three consecutive tiles. He then discards as normal, and play continues to his right.

Those are the only three legal ways to claim a discard. Also keep in mind that only the most recently discarded tile may ever be claimed for any reason.

Declaring Mahjong

A Mahjong is a hand consisting of four sets and a pair. In simple scoring, that's all you need. Under International Scoring, Mahjong can only be declared if your hand is worth at least 8 points (see Chapter 4). However, like every rule in Mahjong, there are exceptions for International Scoring:

- **Chicken Hand**—If your four sets and a pair are worth 0 points, this is called a Chicken Hand, and is actually worth 8 points! Be careful though, because even a single point will invalidate this hand, and single points are hard to avoid (as you'll see in Chapter 4).
- **Special Hands**—There are also a few special hands that count as a valid scoring Mahjong even though they do not consist of four sets and a pair. These either consist of Knitted Tiles, Seven Pairs, or Thirteen Orphans, and will be discussed in more detail in Chapter 4. For now, it's fine to just think of Mahjong as four sets and a pair.

In any case, once a player has the necessary tiles to make a Mahjong and at least 8 points, they may declare Mahjong!

There are four ways the hand can end:

1. **Win by self-draw.** A player draws the last tile they need to make a valid Mahjong from the wall. After drawing the tile from the wall, the player declares Mahjong! and reveals her hand. If it is not a valid Mahjong declaration, that player is out of the game, and play continues for the other three players.

2. **Win by discard.** The tile a player needs is discarded by someone else. The player immediately declares Mahjong, picks up the tile, and reveals her hand. If it is not a valid Mahjong declaration, that player is out of the game, and play continues for the other three players.

3. **Robbing the Kong.** This is a special action you can take when you have a *ready hand* (a hand needing only one more tile to achieve Mahjong) and another player is attempting to improve his Melded Pung into a Melded Kong with a fourth identical tile. If that tile would give you Mahjong, you may say "Mahjong" and steal the tile from the other player. This is called Stealing the Kong, Robbing the Kong, or sometimes Scratching the Kong. You then reveal your winning hand as normal. (Note that you can only rob a Kong that is specifically being improved from a Melded Pung. You cannot rob a newly created Concealed Kong.)

4. **Wall Game.** If a player starts their turn and there are no tiles left to draw from the wall, the hand ends with no winner.

Scoring the Hand

The player who declares Mahjong is the only one who will score any points. First, the player declaring Mahjong reveals her hand and tallies the total value using the scoring guide in Chapter 4.

If the total is fewer than 8 points (not including bonus tiles), the declaring player has incorrectly declared Mahjong, and must pay a penalty of 10 points to each player. (It is recommended to ignore this rule for your first few games while you are learning the ropes.) Either way, if the Mahjong is incorrect, then the wrongly declaring player is removed from the game until it is time to pay the winner, and play continues with the other three players.

Presuming the declaring player has indeed achieved a legal Mahjong, it is time for scoring and payment. Score the hand according to the scoring guide in Chapter 4, and receive payouts as follows:

- If the Mahjong was a self-drawn win, each player pays the winner 8 points plus the total value of the winning hand.
- If the Mahjong was a win by discard, the discarding player pays the winner 8 points plus the total value of the winning hand, while the other two players pay only 8 points each to the winner.
- If the Mahjong occurred by Robbing the Kong, the player who was robbed pays the winner 8 points plus the total value of the winning hand, while the other two players pay only 8 points each to the winner.
- If the hand ends in a Wall Game, no payouts take place, because there is no winner.
- After the hand ends, all tiles are pushed into the center and mixed up again, and the deal passes to the next player (see the "Rounds and Prevailing Winds" section earlier in this chapter). Once all sixteen hands are complete, point totals are calculated, and payments are made if players are playing for money.

Only the winning player who has declared Mahjong may score any points. That player reveals her hand face-up, and tallies her score (allowing the other players to double-check and verify). A common method for doing this is to use the discarded tile pool to count points, using face-down tiles as 10 points each, and face-up tiles as 1 point each.

CHAPTER 4

INTERNATIONAL MAHJONG – SCORING

While the gameplay of International Mahjong may be relatively simple to understand, the scoring is somewhat complex. This chapter has the full International Mahjong Scoring Rules, as well as Primary Rules (a modified form of official tournament rules, with fewer hands), Simple Rules (an unofficial variant to learn the concepts of scoring), and Casual Rules (for players who just want to learn the gameplay and not score).

Simple Scoring

If you are learning Mahjong for the very first time, the 81 fans of International Scoring (or even the 30 fans of International Scoring) may be a little bit overwhelming for your first game, and so you may wish to use the simple scoring variant. It is as follows:

- Four Chows (all runs, no Pungs/Kongs)—2 points
- Four Pungs/Kongs (all of a kind, no Chows)—6 points
- Single Dragon Pung/Kong—2 points
- Two Dragon Pungs/Kongs—6 points (do not also score 2 points for single Dragon Pung)
- Seated Wind Pung/Kong (set of the Wind that matches your current seat, e.g., East for the dealer)—2 points
- Flower/Season tile—1 point each
- Win by self-draw (not win by discard)—1 point

Although it skips over most of the complexities of International Scoring, the simple scoring will teach you the value of Dragon Pungs, that Pungs are generally worth more than Chows, the bonus points for Seated Wind, and that the circumstances in which you get your last tile matter.

Simple scoring has no point minimum for declaring Mahjong, so you may well declare Mahjong on a hand that has only a single point for the one Flower you drew, and no other points for your two Chows and two Pungs. That's fine; thanks to the 8-point victory bonus, you'll still collect some points from your opponents whenever you win.

Casual/Win-or-Lose Scoring

For players who have difficulty memorizing or poring over dozens of special scoring hands, or for players who prefer a more casual approach to the game, or especially for new players attempting to learn the basics of Mahjong, the casual scoring system can be a relaxing way to play Mahjong. If you find that you are not yet ready to worry about points, this is the scoring variant for you.

There are no special hands or points in this casual gameplay, and consequently no minimum-point barrier to Mahjong and no choosing of hands, and the only benefit of Flowers and Kongs is getting to draw a replacement tile. Tiles may be called from the discards as normal, and the first player to get four sets (Chows/Pungs/Kongs) and a pair declares Mahjong and is the winner. This scoring method does make for a much less interesting game, so you probably won't play it much once you learn

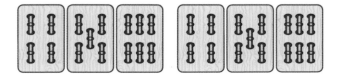

HAND 4.1

PART 2. INTERNATIONAL MAHJONG

the full rules, but if you want to practice the basic gameplay before getting into lists of scoring fans, try a casual win-or-lose game.

International Scoring

The International Rules for scoring are somewhat more complex, and consist of a large number of fans (particular combinations of tiles or conditions) that are added together to calculate your score. The International Competition Rules include 81 fans worth anywhere from 1 to 88 points. Newer players will most likely prefer to start with the International Primary Rules, which use a more manageable 30 fans ranging from 1 to 24 points. Remember that under International Rules, your hand must be worth 8 points *not including bonus tiles* (Flowers/Seasons) in order to declare Mahjong.

There are five principles of scoring, which will help you figure out how many points your hand is worth.

Principle 1: Non-Repeat Principle

When a fan is included in, or implied by, another fan, only the most valuable fan is scored (see **HAND 4.1**).

For example, if you scored 24 points for "Pure Triple Chow" (three Chows of the same number and suit, e.g., Bam4, Bam5, Bam6), you would not score an additional point for "Pure Double Chow" (two Chows of the same number and suit), because you could never have a Triple Chow without a Double Chow.

Principle 2: Non-Separation Principle

After combining sets to create a fan, you cannot rearrange those sets to create other fans. For example, let's go back to the first hand discussed, that had three copies each of Bam4, Bam5, Bam6. You can score that as a Pure Triple Chow, for 24 points. You may notice that because you have three copies each of Bam4, Bam5, Bam6, you could have instead rearranged them to score Pure Shifted Pungs, also for 24 points. But once you have scored either one of these fans, your tiles are locked in the sets you used to score, and may not be rearranged to form other ones (see **HAND 4.1**).

Principle 3: Non-Identical Principle

Once you use a set to create a fan, you may not combine it with other sets to create the same fan (see **HAND 4.1**).

Let's return to your example hand. Bam123 and Bam456 is two consecutive Chows, which is a Short Straight for 1 point. You have a trio of Bam456 Chows, so it might be tempting to claim three Short Straights. But because you have already used your Bam123 Chow to score a Short Straight, you cannot use the same set for the same fan. If you had two Bam123, two Bam456, only then could you score two Short Straights.

Principle 4: Freedom to Choose
(High versus Low Principle)

If a set could be used to form either a higher-scoring or lower-scoring fan, the player is allowed to choose the higher-scoring fan.

If you recall, our example hand could be arranged either to form Pure Triple Chow or Pure Shifted Pungs. In this case, both fans are worth the same 24 points, but if you imagine that one of those fans were worth more than the other, you would be allowed to choose the higher-scoring fan. Likewise, you are allowed to claim Pure Triple Chow instead of Pure Double Chow, since your example hand qualifies for either.

Principle 5: Exclusionary Rule
(Account-Once Principle)

Once you have combined some sets to create a fan, you can only combine any remaining sets once with a set that has already been used.

This one is slightly tricky to understand, but basically means that you always want to score your highest-value fan first, because any sets outside that fan can only be used once with sets in that fan. Let's imagine a slightly different example hand: Bam123, Bam123, Bam456, Bam456, Crak55. You can use the entire hand to score points for "No Honor Tiles" (No Dragons/Winds), and another point for "One Voided Suit" (No Dots). Nothing is outside those fans, because they use the whole hand, so you're fine so far.

Now let's take 1 point for Short Straight for your first set of Bam123, and first set of Bam456. The remaining two sets can only be used once with any used set. So you take the second set of Bam123, combining it with the first Bam123 for 1 point for Pure Double Chow. The only remaining set is the second Bam456. You could either combine it with the second Bam123 for a second Short Straight, or combine it with the first Bam456 for a second Pure Double Chow. But you *cannot* do both at once, because that remaining second Bam123 can only be used once with a set that has already been used, a category into which all other sets in your hand already fall.

Scoring a Sample Hand

Let's practice scoring the hand used as an example for most of this chapter (see **HAND 4.1**).

You want to score your best fan first, so looking in the 24-point section of International Scoring, your choices are either Pure Triple Chow (a trio of Bam456) or Pure Shifted Pungs (Bam444, Bam555, Bam666). You can't score both, because of the non-separation rule defined by Principle 2. The points for either option seem to be the same. However, since your remaining set of Bam123 is a Chow, you'd rather have the rest of your hand also be Chows, and your freedom to choose, as outlined in Principle 4, gives you that option—as well as the option to score the Pure Triple Chow instead of the Pure Double Chow (you can't score both because of the non-repeat rule enshrined in Principle 1).

So you take 24 points for your Pure Triple Chow. Thanks to your choice earlier, you can then grab 2 bonus points for All Chows. You'll also pick up another bonus point for No Honor Tiles, and another for One Voided Suit. That brings your total to 28 points.

But you're not quite done yet. You still have an unused Bam123 Chow. You can match it with any of your Bam456 Chows for a Short Straight, which is worth 1 more point. Sadly, you can only do so once—the non-identical rule of Principle 3 prevents you from using the same Bam123 to make multiple Short Straights. And even if it did not, the exclusionary rule of Principle 5 means that your remaining Bam123 set could only be used once with sets already included in the 24-point fan anyway.

So, your total score for this hand would be 29—plus any points you might have received for how you claimed the winning tile, or bonus points for Flower tiles. Let's pretend you drew the winning tile off the wall (self-drawn for 1 point), and had two Flower tiles (1 point each). That brings your hand total to 32.

Now it's time to collect your winnings from the other players! Because you won on self-draw, you'll be getting the full payment from everyone, not just a discarder. You add the 8-point victory bonus to your 32-point hand to get a total of 40. You demand that from each player, so the other three players will each be down 40 points, and you'll be up a cool 120. You've just scored your first Mahjong hand.

Primary Scoring Fans

The 81 fans of the full International Competition Scoring rubric can be a lot to learn, especially if you're new to Mahjong as a whole. That's why the World Mahjong Organization created the International Mahjong Primary Competition Rules. Think of it as a primary school for learning International Mahjong. Instead of 81 fans, you only have to learn 30, and the range of points is much smaller.

Because of this, the minimum score to declare Mahjong using the Primary Rules is *only 6 points*, instead of the standard 8 points required for full International Rules. This is an important change to remember, because due to reduced point values, it would be even more difficult to achieve 8 points in Primary Scoring.

In addition, the final scoring payouts are slightly different in the Primary Rules. On a win by self-draw, each player pays the winning player the exact value of the winning hand, as scored using the following chart. On a win by discard, only the discarding player pays the winner the value of the hand, and the other two players do not pay.

There are four 1-point hands, six 2-point hands, two 4-point hands, five 6-point hands, four 8-point hands, four 12-point hands, three 16-point hands, and two 24-point hands. Here they are, in ascending point order:

1-POINT HANDS

Melded Kong (Pung)	A Kong (four of a kind) finished by claiming a discard or promoted from a Melded Pung.
One Voided Suit (Suit)	The hand only contains two of the three main suits (Dots, Bams, Craks) and no tiles from the third suit.
No Honors (Suit)	The hand is made entirely of suited tiles, and contains no Honors (Winds or Dragons).
Flower Tiles (Special)	Each Flower/Season tile is worth 1 point, but these points do not count toward the 6-point minimum to declare Mahjong.

2-POINT HANDS

Dragon Pung (Pung)	A Pung (or Kong) of Dragon tiles.
Concealed Hand (Wait)	Concealed Hand (no melded sets), win by discard.
Tile Hog (Special)	Using all four of a tile without using them as a Kong (e.g., Bam111, Bam123).
Double Pung (Pung)	Two Pungs (or Kongs) of the same number in two different suits.
Two Concealed Pungs (Pung)	Two Pungs that are not melded.
Concealed Kong (Pung)	Four identical tiles, declared as a Kong, all self-drawn (no discard claims).

4-POINT HANDS

Fully Concealed Hand (Wait)	Concealed Hand (no melded sets), win by self-draw.
Last Tile (Wait)	Winning with a tile that is the last of the four copies in the game. This can only be claimed when the other three copies are visible to all players, meaning that they have been discarded, melded face-up, or are elsewhere in the winning hand (turned face-up on scoring).

6-POINT HANDS

All Pungs (Pung)	Hand consists of four Pungs/Kongs and a pair.
Half Flush (Suit)	Hand is void of two suits, consisting only of Honor tiles and a single suit (e.g., all Bams and Wind tiles—though note that if there are no Honor tiles at all, this becomes the 24-point Full Flush).
Mixed Shifted Chows (Chow)	Three Chows, one in each suit, each starting one higher than the next (e.g., Bam234, Dot345, Crak456).
All Types (Suit)	Hand where all five types are represented among four sets and the pair (e.g., Bam123, Dot222, Crak456, NNN, DD).
Two Dragon Pungs (Honor)	Two Pungs (or Kongs) of Dragon tiles.

8-POINT HANDS

Mixed Straight (Chow)	A Full Straight formed by consecutive Chows of all three suits (e.g., Bam123, Dot456, Crak789).
Mixed Triple Chow (Chow)	Three Chows of the same numbers, one in each suit (e.g., Bam234, Dot234, Crak234).
Out with Replacement Tile (Wait)	Win after melding a Kong and drawing your replacement tile as the last tile you need for Mahjong. Note: this does not apply for replacement tiles from Flowers, only from Kongs.
Robbing the Kong (Wait)	Win by Robbing the Kong, claiming a tile another player is attempting to add to a Melded Pung to upgrade it to a Kong.

12-POINT HANDS

Upper Four (Suits)	Hand contains only 6 through 9 in standard suits.
Lower Four (Suits)	Hand contains only 1 through 4 in standard suits.
Big Three Winds (Honors)	Hand includes three Pungs of Winds.
Lesser Honors and Knitted Tiles (Special)	A hand made up of single tiles (no pairs allowed) that are either Honor tiles or are part of a different Knitted Sequence in each suit. A Knitted Sequence is either 147, 258, or 369 (e.g., Dot147, Crak25, Bam369, NWE, Green Dragon, Red Dragon, White Dragon).

16-POINT HANDS

Pure Straight (Chow)	Hand includes 1 through 9 in the same suit, in three consecutive Chows (e.g., Bam123, Bam456, Bam789).
Pure Shifted Chows (Chow)	Three Chows in the same suit, each starting one number higher or each starting two numbers higher (e.g., Bam123, Bam345, Bam567).
All Fives (Suit)	Four sets and a pair that each contain at least one 5 (e.g., Bam345, Bam567, Crak555, Dot456, Dot55).

24-POINT HANDS

Full Flush (Suit)	The entire hand, including all four sets and the pair, uses only tiles from a single suit, and no Honors (e.g., Dot111, Dot234, Dot456, Dot999, Dot77).
Seven Pairs (Special)	A hand made up of seven pairs.

Those are the 30 fans for Primary Rules. Here they are organized by type:

HONORS (PUNGS WITH HONORS)

Dragon Pung	2 points
Two Dragon Pungs	6 points
Big Three Winds	12 points

PUNGS AND KONGS

Melded Kong	1 point
Double Pung	2 points
Two Concealed Pungs	2 points
Concealed Kong	2 points
All Pungs	6 points

CHOWS

Mixed Shifted Chow	6 points
Mixed Straight	8 points
Mixed Triple Chow	8 points
Pure Straight	16 points
Pure Shifted Chows	16 points

SUITS

One Voided Suit	1 point
No Honors	1 point
Half Flush	6 points
All Types	6 points
Upper Four	12 points
Lower Four	12 points
All Fives	16 points
Full Flush	24 points

WAIT	
Concealed Hand	2 points
Fully Concealed Hand	4 points
Last Tile	4 points
Out with Replacement Tile	8 points
Robbing the Kong	8 points

SPECIAL	
Flower Tiles	1 point each
Tile Hog	2 points
Lesser Honors and Knitted Tiles	12 points
Seven Pairs	24 points

International Scoring Fans

Here are the 81 fans with which you can score. They have been grouped by ascending point value, so that the thirteen 1-point hands are first, followed by the ten 2-point hands, the four 4-point hands, the six 6-point hands, the ten 8-point hands, the five 12-point hands, the six 16-point hands, the nine 24-point hands, the three 32-point hands, the two 48-point hands, the six 64-point hands, and finally the seven 88-point hands.

It is also worth noting the different types of fans. Nearly half of them are based on Pungs/Kongs or Chows. There are also a number based on suits, Honor tiles, and Terminals. Finally, there are nine special hands that follow their own rules, as well as a dozen fans based on how you were waiting for your last tile. After the full scoring breakdown, you'll see a short summary list sorted by type. But first, here they are sorted by points, with the most common hands listed first.

1-POINT FANS

Pure Double Chow (Chow)	Two Chows of the same suit and number (e.g., Dot567, Dot567).
Mixed Double Chow (Chow)	Two Chows of the same number but different suit (e.g., Dot567, Bam567).
Short Straight (Chow)	Two consecutive Chows in the same suit (e.g., Crak234, Crak567).
Two Terminal Chows (Chow)	Chows of 123 and 789 in the same suit (e.g., Bam123, Bam789).
Pung of Terminals or Honors (Honors)	Pung of 1s, 9s, or Off-Winds (e.g., Crak111).
Melded Kong (Kong)	A Kong claimed by picking up a discard, or promoted from a Melded Pung (four of a kind).
One Voided Suit (Suits)	A hand that is missing one of the three main suits (Dots, Bams, or Craks).
No Honors (Suits)	A hand that contains only the three main suits (no Winds or Dragons).
Edge Wait (Wait)	A hand waiting on the inner edge of a Terminal Chow, when that is the only tile that will complete the hand. In other words, the last tile needed to complete Mahjong is either a 3 to complete a 1-2-3 Chow, or a 7 to complete a 7-8-9 Chow. Note that if the hand could be formed in a different way to finish with a different final tile, this fan cannot be scored.
Closed Wait (Wait)	A hand waiting for the middle tile of a Chow, when that is the only tile that will complete the hand (e.g., holding a Bam4, Bam6, and needing a Bam5, to complete the Chow and the Mahjong). Note that if the hand could be formed in a different way to finish with a different final tile, this fan cannot be scored.

1-POINT FANS (continued)

Closed Wait (Wait)	A hand waiting for the second tile of a pair, when that is the only tile that will complete the hand. Note that if the hand could be formed in a different way to finish with a different final tile, this fan cannot be scored.
Self-Drawn (Wait)	Declaring Mahjong with a self-drawn win. The final tile that creates Mahjong is taken from the wall (instead of being called from a discard).
Flower/Season Bonus Tiles (Special)	Each Flower or Season tile is immediately set aside when drawn, and a replacement tile is drawn. They are worth 1 point each at the end of the game, but do *not* count toward the 8-point minimum for a player to declare Mahjong.

2-POINT FANS

Dragon Pung (Honors)	A Pung (or Kong) of Dragon tiles (three of the same color of dragon).
Pung of Prevailing Wind (Honors)	A Pung (or Kong) of the Prevailing Wind. Remember, the Prevailing Wind only chances once every four hands.
Pung of Seat Wind (Honors)	A Pung (or Kong) of the declaring player's Seat Wind (e.g., for the dealer, East, this would be a Pung of East Winds). Note that if a Wind is neither the Prevailing Wind nor your Seat Wind, it is counted as the single point fan Pung of Honors.
Concealed Hand (Wait)	Hand without any melded (revealed) sets, which is won off another player's discard. Note that if the hand is won by self-draw, it instead becomes the 4-point Fully Concealed Hand.
All Chows (Chow)	A hand consisting of four sets of Chow, with the pair made from one of the three main suits (no Honor tiles).

2-POINT FANS (continued)

Tile Hog (Special)	A hand that includes all four of a suited tile, but does not use them as a Kong (e.g., a Pung of Bam333 and a Chow of Bam345).
Double Pung (Pung)	Two Pungs of the same number, in different suits (e.g., Bam555, Dot555).
Two Concealed Pungs (Pung)	Hand includes two Concealed (non-melded) Pungs.
Concealed Kong (Kong)	Hand includes one Concealed (facedown) Kong.
All Simples (Suit)	Hand has no Terminal or Honor tiles. In other words, a hand containing only suited numbers from 2 through 8.

4-POINT FANS

Outside Hand (Honors)	Each of the four sets, and the pair, contains at least one Terminal or Honor (e.g., Dot123, Crak789, Bam111, EEE, DD).
Fully Concealed Hand (Wait)	Hand contains only concealed sets (nothing melded), and is won by self-draw. Note that if the hand is won by discard, it instead becomes the 2-point Concealed Hand.
Two Kongs (Kong)	Hand includes two Kongs melded on the table. Note that if a Kong is melded facedown, it is still considered concealed, so you may also score points for Concealed Kong.
Last Tile (Wait)	Winning with a tile that is the last of the four copies in the game. This can only be claimed when the other three copies are visible to all players, meaning that they have been discarded, melded face-up, or are elsewhere in the winning hand (turned face-up on scoring).

6-POINT FANS

All Pungs (Pung)	Hand of four Pungs/Kongs and a pair.
Half Flush (Suit)	Hand is void of two suits, consisting only of Honor tiles and a single suit (e.g., all Bams and Wind tiles). Note that if there are no Honor tiles at all, this becomes the 24-point Full Flush.
Mixed Shifted Chows (Chow)	Three Chows, one in each suit, each starting one higher than the next (e.g., Bam234, Dot345, Crak456).
All Types (Suit)	Hand where all five types are represented among four sets and the pair (e.g., Bam123, Dot222, Crak456, NNN, DD).
Melded Hand (Wait)	Hand that contains four melded sets, and is won by discard.
Two Dragon Pungs (Honor)	Two Pungs (or Kongs) of Dragon tiles.

8-POINT FANS

Mixed Straight (Chow)	A Full Straight formed by consecutive Chows of all three suits (e.g., Bam123, Dot456, Crak789).
Reversible Tiles (Special)	A hand of four sets and a pair that only uses tiles that look the same upside-down. These are Bam245689, Dot1234589, and White Dragon.
Mixed Triple Chow (Chow)	Three Chows of the same numbers, one in each suit (e.g., Bam234, Dot234, Crak234).
Mixed Shifted Pungs (Pung)	Three Pungs (or Kongs) of adjacent numbers, one in each suit (e.g., Bam222, Dot333, Crak444).
Chicken Hand (Special)	A hand that would otherwise score zero points. Flower/Season bonus tile points do not count against this, but any other points will invalidate the Chicken Hand.

8-POINT FANS (continued)

Last Tile Draw (Wait)	Win on self-draw by drawing the last tile in the game, emptying the wall.
Last Tile Claim (Wait)	Win on discard when the player who drew the last tile in the game discards the final tile of the game.
Out with Replacement Tile (Wait)	Win after melding a Kong and drawing your replacement tile as the last tile you need for Mahjong. Note that this does not apply for replacement tiles from Flowers, only from Kongs.
Two Concealed Kongs (Kong)	Have two Concealed (facedown) Kongs.
Robbing the Kong (Wait)	Win by Robbing the Kong, claiming a tile another player is attempting to add to a Melded Pung to upgrade it to a Kong.

12-POINT FANS

Lesser Honors and Knitted Tiles (Special)	A hand made up of single tiles (no pairs allowed) that are either Honor tiles or part of a different Knitted Sequence in each suit. A Knitted Sequence is either 147, 258, or 369 (e.g., Dot147, Crak25, Bam369, NWE, Green Dragon, Red Dragon, White Dragon).
Knitted Straight (Special)	Hand that has one regular set, one pair, and a Knitted Straight, which is three full knitted sets, one in each suit, which combine to make a 1 through 9 Straight (e.g., Bam147, Dot258, Crak369, NNN, DD).
Upper Four (Suits)	Hand contains only 6 through 9 in standard suits.
Lower Four (Suits)	Hand contains only 1 through 4 in standard suits.
Big Three Winds (Honors)	Hand includes three Pungs of Winds.

16-POINT FANS

Pure Straight (Chow)	Hand includes 1 through 9 in the same suit, in three consecutive Chows (e.g., Bam123, Bam456, Bam789).
Three-Suited Terminal Chows (Chow)	Hand of four Chows, which are 123789 in two different suits, and a pair of 5s in the third suit (e.g., Bam123, Bam789, Dot123, Dot789, Crak55).
Pure Shifted Chows (Chow)	Three Chows in the same suit, each starting one number higher or each starting two numbers higher (e.g., Bam123, Bam345, Bam567).
All Fives (Suit)	Four sets and a pair that each contain at least one 5 (e.g., Bam345, Bam567, Crak555, Dot456, Dot55).
Triple Pung (Pung)	Three Pungs (or Kongs) of the same number, one in each suit (e.g., Bam555, Dot555, Crak555).
Three Concealed Pungs (Pung)	Three Concealed Pungs (or Kongs).

24-POINT FANS

Seven Pairs (Special)	A hand made up of seven pairs.
Greater Honors and Knitted Tiles (Special)	A hand made up of single tiles (no pairs allowed), including one of each Dragon, one of each Wind, and seven suited tiles each belonging to a different Knitted Sequence (read: 1-4-7, 2-5-8, and 3-6-9, each trio in a different suit). One example hand might be Bam47, Crak258, Dot36, ESNW, Green Dragon, Red Dragon, White Dragon.
All Even (Pung)	A hand made of all Pungs (or Kongs) of 2s, 4s, 6s, and 8s, as well as a pair of 2s, 4s, 6s, or 8s (e.g., Bam222, Dot444, Crak4444, Dot666, Bam88).

24-POINT FANS (continued)

Full Flush (Suit)	The entire hand, including all four sets and the pair, uses only tiles from a single suit, and no Honors (e.g., Dot111, Dot234, Dot456, Dot999, Dot77).
Pure Triple Chow (Chow)	Three Chows of the same numbers and suit (e.g., Bam345, Bam345, Bam345).
Pure Shifted Pungs (Pung)	Three Pungs (or Kongs) of the same suit, each one higher than the last (e.g., Dot333, Dot444, Dot555).
Upper Tiles (Suit)	Hand of four sets and a pair, all using only 7s, 8s, and 9s from the main three suits, and no Honors (e.g., Dot777, Bam777, Crak789, Bam999, Dot88).
Middle Tiles (Suit)	Hand of four sets and a pair, all using only 4s, 5s, and 6s from the main three suits, and no Honors (e.g., Dot444, Bam444, Crak456, Bam666, Dot55).
Lower Tiles (Suit)	Hand of four sets and a pair, all using only 1s, 2s, and 3s from the main three suits, and no Honors (e.g., Dot111, Bam222, Bam123, Crak123, Dot22).

32-POINT FANS

Four Shifted Chows (Chows)	Four Chows in the same suit, each starting one number higher or each starting two numbers higher (e.g., Bam123, Bam234, Bam345, Bam456).
Three Kongs (Kongs)	Hand includes three Kongs.
All Terminals and Honors (Honors)	Four Pungs/Kongs and a pair, all using only Terminals (1s and 9s) and/or Honor tiles (Dragons and Winds).

48-POINT FANS

Quadruple Chow (Chow)	Four identical Chows (in number and suit) and a pair (e.g., Dot456, Dot456, Dot456, Dot456, Crak22).
Four Pure Shifted Pungs (Pung)	Four Pungs (or Kongs) of the same suit, each one higher than the last (e.g., Dot333, Dot444, Dot555, Dot666).

64-POINT FANS

All Terminals (Honors)	Four Pungs (or Kongs) and a pair, consisting only of 1s and 9s in the three basic suits.
Little Four Winds (Honors)	Three Pungs (or Kongs) of Winds (and any one other set), and a pair of the fourth Wind.
Little Three Dragons (Honors)	Two Pungs of Dragons (and any two other sets), and a pair of the third Dragon.
All Honors (Honors)	Four Pungs (or Kongs) of Honor tiles, as well as a pair of Honor tiles.
Four Concealed Pungs (Pungs)	Four Concealed Pungs (or Kongs), and a pair.
Pure Terminal Chows (Chow)	Hand made of 123, 123, 789, 789, 55, all in a single suit.

88-POINT FANS

Big Four Winds (Honors)	A Pung (or Kong) of each of the four Winds, along with any pair.
Big Three Dragons (Honors)	A Pung (or Kong) of each of the three Dragons, along with any other set, and any pair.
All Green (Special)	Hand consisting of four sets and a pair made only from purely green tiles (Bam23468, Green Dragon).
Nine Gates (Wait)	*Before* drawing the final tile for Mahjong, this hand must be 1112345678999 in a single suit. It is so named because there are nine different tiles in the suit (1 through 9) that will complete a valid Mahjong.

Four Kongs (Kongs)	Four Kongs and a pair.
Seven Shifted Pairs (Special)	A special hand consisting of seven pairs of the same suit, of consecutive numbers (e.g., Bam22, Bam33, Bam44, Bam55, Bam66, Bam77, Bam88).
Thirteen Orphans (Special)	A special hand consisting of one of each Terminal and Honor tile, and an additional matching tile for any (e.g., Bam19, Dot19, Crak19, ESWNN, Red Dragon, Green Dragon, White Dragon).

If you already have a set or two in your hand and want to know where it can go, here are the scoring hands sorted by type:

HONOR TILES

Note that because Honor tiles have no numbers to make Chows, any sets made with Honor tiles will always be Pungs or Kongs.

Off-Wind Pung	1 point
Dragon Pung	2 points
Prevailing Wind Pung	2 points
Seat Wind Pung	2 points
Two Dragons	6 points
Big Three Winds	12 points
Little Four Winds	64 points
Little Three Dragons	64 points
All Honors	64 points
Big Four Winds	88 points
Big Three Dragons	88 points

PUNGS AND KONGS

Terminal Pung	1 point
Melded Kong	1 point
Double Pung	2 points
Two Concealed Pungs	2 points
Concealed Kong	2 points
Two Kongs	4 points
All Pungs	6 points
Mixed Shifted Pungs	8 points
Triple Pung	16 points
Three Concealed Pungs	16 points
All Even	24 points
Pure Shifted Pungs	24 points
Three Kongs	32 points
All Terminals and Honors	32 points
Four Pure Shifted Pungs	48 points
Four Concealed Pungs	64 points
All Terminals	64 points
Four Kongs	88 points

CHOWS

Pure Double Chow	1 point
Mixed Double Chow	1 point
Short Straight	1 point
Two Terminal Chows	1 point
All Chows	2 points
Mixed Shifted Chows	6 points
Mixed Straight	8 points
Mixed Triple Chow	8 points
Knitted Straight	12 points

CHOWS (continued)

Pure Straight	16 points
Three Suit Terminal Chows	16 points
Pure Shifted Chows	16 points
Pure Triple Chow	24 points
Four Shifted Chows	32 points
Quadruple Chow	48 points
Pure Terminal Chows	64 points

TERMINAL HANDS

Terminal Pung	1 point
All Simples	2 points
Outside Hand	4 points
Upper Four	12 points
Lower Four	12 points
All Fives	16 points
Three Suit Terminal Chows	16 points
Upper Tiles	24 points
Middle Tiles	24 points
Lower Tiles	24 points
Pure Terminal Chows	64 points

SUITS

One Voided Suit	1 point
No Honors	1 point
Half Flush	6 points
All Types	6 points
Full Flush	24 points
All Green	88 points
Nine Gates	88 points

SPECIAL HANDS

Flower/Season Tiles	1 point each*
Tile Hog	2 points
Reversible Tiles	8 points
Chicken Hand	8 points
Knitted Straight	12 points
Lesser Honors, Knitted Tiles	12 points
Greater Honors, Knitted Tiles	24 points
Seven Pairs	24 points
Seven Shifted Pairs	88 points
Thirteen Orphans	88 points

*Does not count toward 8-point minimum.

WAIT HANDS/GOING OUT

Edge Wait	1 point
Closed Wait	1 point
Single Wait	1 point
Self-Drawn Win	1 point
Concealed Hand	2 points
Fully Concealed Hand	4 points
Last Tile	4 points
Melded Hand	6 points
Last Tile Draw	8 points
Last Tile Claim	8 points
Out with the Replacement Tile	8 points
Robbing the Kong	8 points

CHAPTER 5

INTERNATIONAL MAHJONG— STRATEGY

Now we get into the most interesting part of Mahjong: the strategy! Because Mahjong is a game of luck, and because a lot depends on your opponents, there is no guaranteed winning strategy. However, there are certainly a number of strategies you can use to improve your odds of victory, from deciding what hands to aim for, to knowing when to pick up a discarded tile.

Evaluating Your Opening Hand

You've sat down and chosen a dealer, the tiles have been shuffled, the wall has been built, and you have received a hand of tiles. The first thing you'll want to do is arrange your hand. This will make it much easier for you to analyze your tiles and figure out the best play strategy. Most players prefer to organize their hand by suits first, and then by numbers ascending within the suit. In other words, you could put all your Bamboos on the left, followed by Circles, then Characters, then Winds, then Dragons. A sample hand you might be dealt, arranged by suit, follows (see **HAND 5.1**).

You aren't required to arrange your hand this way, but the reason this traditional arrangement is popular is because it makes it easy to evaluate your hand at a glance. The arrangement is also especially helpful as you are learning the game, allowing you to see the combinations as they form.

That being said, it is generally a bad idea to separate your tiles into groups (e.g., by Pungs, Chows, pairs, and so on), as this can give away valuable information to your opponents. Some players will even put tiles into false groups and/or arrange their hand in random order instead of by suit, to deliberately mislead opponents. You probably don't need to go this far, especially when you are learning, but grouping tiles into Pungs and Chows should still be avoided.

It is true that if you always have your tiles in the same order, an opponent could theoretically note where in your hand you placed a tile taken from the wall, and effectively guess what type of tile it is, or note from where in your hand you pulled your discards to gather information about your hand. But if you're just playing casually and not betting serious money, you probably don't need to worry about it—and it's worth keeping your hand in suit order, especially while you're learning!

Once you've arranged your hand, it's time to start thinking about what direction to try to go with your opening hand. One of the trickier parts of International Mahjong is that it is a mixed scoring system with a minimum-point hand, meaning that you have more freedom than in American Mahjong, which requires specific hands to win, but which is not as open as simple scoring Mahjong where any four sets and a pair will suffice. You need a combination of aiming for certain hands or categories of hands, while simultaneously being open to other opportunities that may appear as the game progresses.

The key to being a good International Mahjong player is flexibility; the hand you set out to make at the beginning may well not be the hand you end up winning with. That being said, the longest of journeys begins with a single step, and certainly your odds of winning are much higher if you make a smart choice about what type of hand to pursue at the beginning of the game.

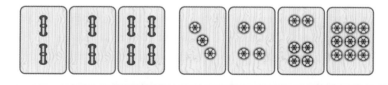

HAND 5.1

PART 2. INTERNATIONAL MAHJONG

The most obvious strategy should almost go without saying, but we'll say it anyway just to be clear: if you're really close to a winning hand, go for that one! All the rest of this strategy section about planning is irrelevant if you are dealt Bam11223345689, EE—all you need is a Bam7 to win with a Pure Straight (and bonus points for All Chows, Half Flush, and Double Chow), so that should be your game plan. Same thing if you're dealt a hand of all Dragons, or twelve of the Thirteen Orphans. The closer you are to your target hand, the better.

Obviously if you can find a good fan, where you're only missing a single tile, you should aim for that one, but most of the time your opening hand will be at least three or four tiles away (if not more) from any winning Mahjong hand, so you'll have to pick a target among the numerous hands that you are still somewhat far from achieving. That is where the strategy of the game comes in.

An important aspect to keep in mind when thinking about what fans you might aim for is that, roughly speaking, the difficulty level of achieving a fan corresponds to its point value. You get 1 point for a Pung of Terminals or Off-Winds, because collecting three of these is not too difficult, especially as they are likely to be thrown away early by other players (as will be discussed later). Meanwhile, a hand of Seven Pairs is worth a full 24 points, which should indicate to you that although making pairs sounds very easy, successfully completing this hand might not be.

While obviously more points are better in a vacuum, nobody plays Mahjong in a vacuum (because it would be hard to breathe). More points for a special fan directly translates to a higher difficulty of achieving it. So

if you are choosing between two hands to pursue and you're not super-close to the difficult hand, as long as you can meet your 8-point minimum with either hand, it's generally better to aim for the lower-value hand, especially as a new player. Remember, it's better to win with an 8-point hand than to lose aiming for a 24-point hand!

That being said, it is *best* to hold on to sets that will let you progress toward multiple hands at once, so you can aim for more points without giving up on a higher-probability win. But if you have to choose one or the other, your best option is to go for the safer bet. Unless you're closer to achieving the high-value hand, aim for the hand that is likely to give you Mahjong faster.

As discussed in Chapter 1, the International Rules were developed by a gathering of Mahjong experts from across the different provinces of China, who debated and refined the rules over a period of two years to make Mahjong an official national sport. So rest assured that the point values were very carefully considered, and that indeed the higher-point hands will be more difficult to achieve.

With some hands, this is fairly obvious: Big Four Winds is an 88-point hand; because of the sixteen Winds in the entire game, it requires you to have at least a dozen of them, with a Pung of each of the four Winds. This means if any other player has even a single pair of any Wind, or if two of the same Wind are in the discards, this hand is literally impossible to make.

It may be less obvious why a hand like Thirteen Orphans is worth 88 points, since you only need a single copy of each tile aside from one pair. That doesn't sound very complicated, until you consider three main points.

1. First of all, you need each of these specific thirteen tiles, which means that if even a single one of those tiles is unavailable (e.g., all the Bam1s are gone because South made a Pung of Bam111, and West has a Chow of Bam123), the hand can never be completed.
2. Second, because these are all singletons and not Pungs or Chows, you cannot claim any of the needed tiles off a discard; you must draw your

entire hand yourself, so if another player discards the fourth Green Dragon midway through the game, you are suddenly out of luck.

3. And third, if for either of these reasons it finally becomes apparent that you cannot complete this hand (which is likely), you have an absolutely terrible bunch of tiles for making anything else, since you have no like tiles.

You may think this information isn't very important, because you'll rarely go for one of the most difficult hands in the game. But knowing *why* it's such a difficult hand to put together will help you understand what makes a hand easier to assemble, and how you might go about evaluating your opening hand.

What Tiles Do You Need?

This is probably the most important consideration no matter what point of the game you're at. Later in the game, you'll see that when deciding what to discard, it's better to build your hand in such a way that multiple tiles with multiple copies would let you win, rather than needing to draw one specific tile that's the last of its type. But it's also an important thing to consider when choosing what hand to go for in the first place.

One thing you'll notice immediately is that if you have two tiles and you need a third to complete a set, you have much better odds if those tiles are in a run than being alike. In other words, if you have Bam22, there are two tiles in the game that will transform that into a legal Pung—the other pair of Bam2s not yet in your hand. You need one of those two tiles to make Bam222. But if instead you are holding Bam23, there are potentially eight tiles that might convert those two tiles into a legal Chow—the four Bam1s, and the four Bam4s. You can make a Chow of Bam123 or Bam234.

This means there are literally *four times* as many tiles that can turn two adjacent simple tiles into a set than there are tiles to turn two identical tiles into a set. You don't have to be a math expert to know that having your chances be four times higher is a good thing. During the game, information might change your calculations, but when choosing your target hand at the beginning of the game, Chows are by far your best odds.

Now of course, because the creators of the International Scoring system realized this, a single Chow is not worth any points, while a Pung of Terminals or Honors is. And this can present a problem, since you'll need 8 points in order to declare Mahjong. But there are some 8-point hands based around Chows that aren't too difficult to make, especially if you start with good tiles.

Where Can You Claim the Tiles You Need?

There are three places you could claim a tile: from the wall, from your left-hand neighbor's discard, and from the other two discards. Any hand or set will let you claim tiles from the wall. If you are completing a Chow, you may also claim tiles from your left-hand neighbor's discard. And if you are completing a Pung/Kong, the discards of all three of your opponents are fair game in addition to the wall.

The result is that special hands (pairs, Knitted Straights, and so on) will be more difficult to achieve because you must draw your needed tiles from the wall. Remember that for any tile in the wall, there's a 75 percent chance that one of your opponents will draw it instead of you! If you're completing a Chow, you can also call the discard of your left-hand opponent, which means if he doesn't need the tile, your odds have improved somewhat. And if you're completing a Pung, you can call the

HAND 5.2

PART 2. INTERNATIONAL MAHJONG

discard from anywhere, which is important when there are only two tiles remaining.

What can you deduce taking this in combination with the first point? You already know that it's easier to complete a Chow of Bam23 than a Pung of Bam22, because there are more tiles available. But what if you consider a Chow that requires the middle number rather than the edges? If you are holding Bam24, the only tile that will complete it is Bam3. So suddenly, there are only half as many options to complete the set as you had with Bam23, where you could use either a Bam1 or a Bam4 (see **HAND 5.2**).

Let's imagine a scenario where your opening hand includes Bam224. Ideally, you'd like to hold on to all three of these tiles, since that would let you complete a set with either a Bam2 to Pung Bam222, or a Bam3 to Chow Bam234. But maybe the rest of your hand is too good to discard, and your fourteenth tile is also one you want to hold on to. In that case, let's imagine that you have to break up your Bam224—which of those two tiles should you discard, Bam2 or Bam4?

You might think discarding Bam2 makes more sense because you learned in the previous point that a Chow is easier to complete than a Pung. And indeed, to your knowledge, there are only two other Bam2s in the game, while there are four available Bam3s, so it seems like your odds would be twice as good if you hold on to Bam24 rather than Bam22.

But what this doesn't take into account is that a Chow can only be called up from your left-hand opponent, while a Pung can be called up from anyone's discard. Let's pretend for the sake of argument that none of your opponents need any Bam2s or Bam3s, and will discard them as

soon as drawn. This means that if a Bam2 is drawn by any player, it can complete your Pung, because either you will draw it off the wall, or one of the other three players will discard it. So of the two copies of that tile that might be pulled from the wall, 100 percent of the time it is drawn, it will complete your set.

Now let's consider the Bam3 you need for a Chow. If you draw it from the wall, you can naturally use it to complete your set. And if your left-hand opponent discards it, you can call it to complete your set. But if your opponent across from you, or your right-hand opponent, discards it, the tile becomes lost to you, because Chows can only be called up from the left-hand opponent's discard! This means that out of the four copies of that tile that might be pulled from the wall, only 50 percent of the time that it is drawn will it be of any use to you, because the other half of the time it will be drawn by a player whose discards you can't use for the Chow.

Naturally, these probabilities are a little more complicated in reality for various reasons, not least of which because your opponents might draw the tile you need and never discard it. But if you just use those numbers as an example, you'll see that 50 percent odds on four tiles is roughly the same probability as 100 percent odds on two tiles, making the chances of drawing your Bam2 and Bam3 pretty much even. Add in the fact that a single tile can turn a Pung into a Kong (which is worth points), and you realize that with similar chances of getting the single tile you need, it might be better to discard the Bam4 and hold the pair of Bam2s.

Then again, you still need to think about the third point of hand evaluation, as this will be most crucial as you look at your opening tiles.

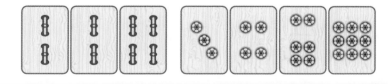

HAND 5.3

How Can You Guarantee Your Point Minimum?

Finally, you've come to the trickiest part of International Mahjong: assembling enough points in fans to reach the 8-point minimum. Now obviously, the first thing to look at is the high-point special hands. As mentioned previously, hands like Knitted Straight and Thirteen Orphans are worth plenty of points to serve as a win if you're close to completing them, but a huge downside (in addition to being difficult to complete) is that they are very inflexible. This means that, generally speaking, you should only pursue them if you already have most of the tiles you need.

Sometimes you will have a less restrictive but still obvious hand, such as being dealt lots of Dragons, which sets you up to try to grab the last few Dragons for lots of points, or even if you only manage Two Dragon Pungs, that still leaves you only needing 2 points from the other eight tiles in your hand, which is easy enough to manage. If you are holding a lot of Honors, it's certainly worth looking at the Honors-based fans to see if you might have enough points just with those, and likewise there are fans that reward you for having all one suit, all high numbers, or all low numbers.

More often, though, your hand will be a bit of a mishmash, containing three or four tiles from each suit, and three or four Honor tiles that are probably not all the same. It is at this point that you have to figure out how to assemble your hand into something that will be worth at least 8 points in fans (see **HAND 5.3**).

Unless you start with a lot of Honor tiles, you are unlikely to reach any of the high-point Honor-based hands. More often, you will be hoping to convert your Honors to Pungs or Kongs for a few points, or even just saving them as a pair to finish out the hand.

But the bulk of your hand is likely going to be suited numbers, and so that will be the most common place to begin looking for how you can build up to 8 points. As previously discussed, Chows are the easiest sets to make, especially when you can be waiting on a tile from either side of your adjacent numbers. For this reason, a single Chow is never worth any points, while a Kong or Honor Pung is.

However, there are plenty of Chow-based hands that are worth enough points to declare Mahjong. The most common one that can stand on its own is Mixed Triple Chow. (There are other Chow hands worth more points, such as Pure Straight and Pure Triple Chow, but these are both less common and easier to spot.) Mixed Triple Chow means having the same three-number Chow run in all three suits, e.g., Bam234, Dot234, Crak234.

Let's look at your hand again (see **HAND 5.3**).

You have a number of tiles toward a Mixed Triple Chow, making that an excellent fan to aim for. In fact, whenever you start a game of Mahjong and have some of the same numbers across different suits, it's worth asking yourself if you can be aiming at a Mixed Triple Chow. As target fans go, Mixed Triple Chow has a number of advantages.

- The biggest advantage of Mixed Triple Chow is that it is an 8-point fan, which means that if you manage to complete it, your hand automatically meets the minimum requirements for Mahjong, so you can make your final set and pair out of whatever is convenient for your tiles.
- While by itself it is worth enough points to cover your Mahjong, a Mixed Triple Chow only uses nine tiles. That means the other two

sets in your hand (a set and a pair) are free to be whatever you like. This has two benefits: not only is the fan easier to complete because you can hold whatever tiles you like in those last four slots as you build the fan, but you can also assemble a set in that slot that gives you another fan when matched with one of the sets already in your Mixed Triple Chow (i.e., if your Mixed Triple Chow ends up being Bam234, Crak234, Dot234, an additional 234 of any suit will add a Pure Double Chow, or any 567 will add a Short Straight, or a Pung and pair of Winds and Dragons will add an All Types).

- A Mixed Triple Chow uses Chows, which are the easiest sets to complete, thus increasing your odds of actually making your Mahjong if you need the same number of tiles as another player waiting on a tougher hand.

- Unlike Pure Triple Chow or Pure Straight (other high-point Chow-based hands), Mixed Triple Chow uses tiles from all three suits. This is convenient because you are likely to start with some tiles in each suit, and gathering all of the tiles in a single suit can be difficult, especially if opponents catch on to what you are doing.

- Mixed Triple Chow is also a very flexible hand. If you start out attempting to form a Mixed Triple Chow, and you don't quite get the tiles you need, you might still be in a very good position to score an 8-point hand in a different way.

Let's look at your example hand again (see **HAND 5.3**). You're four tiles away from two different Mixed Triple Chows. If you draw Bam3, Dot2, Crak34, you have a Mixed Triple Chow of 234. Or if you draw Bam56, Dot5, Crak4, you have a Mixed Triple Chow of 456. So at the beginning of the game, drawing any one of seven different tiles moves you within three tiles of a winning hand—an excellent place to be.

But let's imagine that due to the harsh winds of fate, you are unable to complete your Mixed Triple Chow. You may start well by drawing Bam3 and Crak4, putting you only two tiles away from your 234 Mixed Triple, and upgrading your hand to the following (see **HAND 5.4**).

And then one of your opponents melds a Kong of Dot2. Now you'll never be able to complete Dot234! But no need to panic, because you have a very flexible hand. You'll note that you currently have Bam234 and Crak456. If you can just draw Dot5, you'll also have Dot345, giving you a Mixed Shifted Chow. Mixed Shifted Chow is only worth 6 points instead of 8, so you will need to pick up a pair of points elsewhere, but that shouldn't be too difficult, because you have your other tiles to help you.

If you make your final set another Chow, you can get 2 points for All Chow. If you can get another Green Dragon, you can score 2 points for Dragon Pung. If you haven't called any discarded tiles to complete your Chows, you can score 2 points for Concealed Hand. Or you can try to cobble together a pair of single points for things like a Kong, a Terminal Pung, or No Honors if you drop the Dragons, or Self-Drawn if your

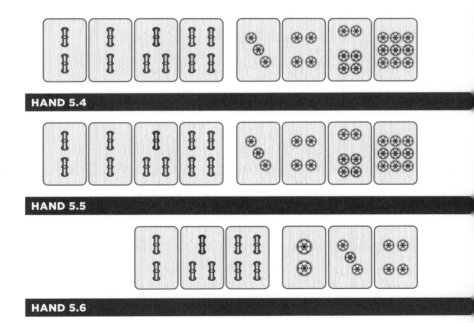

HAND 5.4

HAND 5.5

HAND 5.6

PART 2. INTERNATIONAL MAHJONG

winning tile is self-drawn, or Closed Wait if that elusive Dot5 is the last tile you need, and so on.

But there are many ways you could go with a hand of Chows. It's possible that if you hadn't discarded your East Wind at the beginning, but instead threw away the Crak2 because you weren't insistent on aiming for Crak234, your hand would have ended up looking more like the following (see **HAND 5.5**).

And maybe your Dot5 never comes, but you end up with a Dot2 and a second East Wind. This leaves your hand as the following (see **HAND 5.6**).

This is actually a fine hand, because either a Red Dragon or East Wind will give you Mahjong. Making a Pung out of one of those pairs means that you'd have one set of each type, giving you 6 points for All Types, plus another 1 point for Mixed Double Chow (for the two sets of 234), plus at least 1 point for your Honor Pung (2 if it's the Dragon, or if East is a Prevailing/Seat Wind).

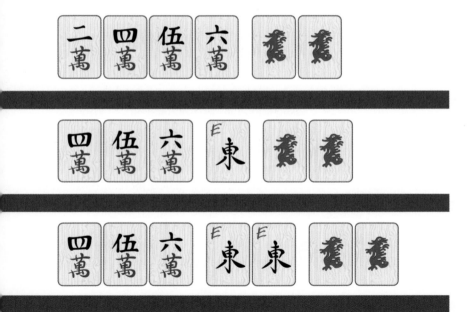

As you can see, aiming for Mixed Triple Chow or Mixed Shifted Chow will give your hand a lot of flexibility, since you will be well positioned to jump to a different winning hand if you don't draw exactly the tiles you had hoped for initially. This can be crucial in a game where you rarely get exactly what you want and when you want it. Of course, this doesn't mean you should always go for Chows. If your hand is set up to make a lot of Pungs, especially if those Pungs share a category (all lower numbers, all upper numbers, all same suit, all Honors), you might be able to make a strong Pung hand, which has the bonus of being able to call anyone's discard. (Chows, remember, can only call the discard of the player to your left.)

Honor Pungs are especially worth discussing, in the context of how many Honors are in your opening hand. As discussed earlier, if you have a lot of Honors, it's easy to make them a mainstay of your hand. Even a pair is always worth holding on to, both because it could become a Pung that's worth points, and because you'll usually need a pair of something to win. But if you have a few singleton Honors, you'll have to decide whether you want to hold on to them or not. The downside of Honors is that they can only be used for Pungs (or the pair), never for Chows, making them slightly less versatile than suited tiles. To make up for this, Pungs of Honors are worth points, making them slightly worthwhile in that respect. But the biggest consideration may be whether you can assemble an All Types hand, as you did in the previous example. The 6 points for an All Types hand will bring you most of the way to Mahjong (or all the way if the Pung is Dragons), meaning that if you have Dragons and Winds in your opening hand, it may be worth trying to collect more of those.

Conversely, if you don't have any Dragons, a single Wind tile is very likely to be useless to you, and you would probably like to replace it with a suited tile—not only because a suited tile is more likely to help you complete a set, but also because you can then grab an extra point for No Honors (or 2 for All Simples). Deciding early on whether you want more Honors or fewer Honors will be crucial in shaping your hand toward

PART 2. INTERNATIONAL MAHJONG

where you want it to be—either one can make a number of winning hands, but you'll need to choose early so you know what to discard.

Strategy During the Game

Now that you've figured out where to go with your opening hand, let's talk about the rest of the game. The three points discussed when picking a target hand are worth keeping in mind throughout the rest of the game:

1. What tiles will I need to win?
   - A hand that can win with three different tiles is better than a hand that needs a specific tile to win.
   - If some of the tiles you need to win are already visible in the discard pile or in an opponent's meld, that's important information.
2. Where will the tiles come from?
   - Do you need tiles for Pungs you can call from anywhere? For Chows that you can only call from one player's discards? Or are you searching for tiles that you must draw yourself?
   - If you can call your needed tile from the discard, will your opponents discard it?
3. What fans can I use these tiles in? How can I be sure to meet the 8-point minimum?
   - A flexible hand is always valuable.

We've talked a lot about the value of keeping your hand flexible, and that's something you should keep in mind throughout the game. Obviously, once you're close to your target hand, you'll likely have to abandon some flexibility in order to pick up the last few tiles you need. But early on, it is useful to keep your hand flexible so you can readjust your target hand based on what you see hit the table.

A common mistake is to become lured by the possibility of a high-point hand, rather than to go in the direction that leaves you the most options. If you are five tiles away from Seven Pairs, but also five tiles away from a Mahjong with Pungs, the Pungs are going to be much easier to complete. This remains true as you draw more tiles, and you might see an opportunity to add a bonus fan to your hand for more points (e.g., by discarding some flexible tiles to go for a Half Flush or All Uppers), when your better move may be to ignore the possibility of extra points in exchange for sitting on a more flexible hand.

Remember, it's better to have two different tiles that will let you win with 10 points, than a route that commits you to only winning with the first tile for 20 points. And you'll realize it as soon as you draw that second tile. But keeping your hand flexible is about more than just your target hand—it's also about what you call from the discard to meld a set.

Don't Meld Too Soon

There are plenty of reasons you *do* want to call up discards for melds, and often melding will be the right call. Aside from the obvious fact that calling a discard for a meld gives you a set and usually moves you closer to a Mahjong hand, calling a Pung is a rare chance to grab the tile of which at most one more (and possibly zero) remains in the game, and if you call a Pung on the discard of your right-hand opponent, you get the bonus of skipping the other two players' turns. So don't hesitate to meld whenever it will help you. Just be aware that it's not always the right choice—especially early in the game.

A common mistake that new players make is to call up any discard that completes a set for them. Why would this be a mistake? Isn't completing sets what you're trying to do? Well, yes. But there are three downsides to calling up a discard.

It Passes Up a Chance to Draw from the Wall

It's possible that the discard is a tile that is only one you sort of need, but the tile you *really* need hasn't been drawn yet. If you call a discard, you're passing your chance to draw the tile you really need from the wall.

And if nothing else, you're also passing up the chance to draw a bonus tile from the wall—remember that these are immediately played and replaced when drawn, so if there's only a single Flower tile on the table, that means seven are still in the wall waiting to be drawn.

Melding a Set Vastly Restricts Your Hand Options

By now you know why a flexible hand is important, because you might draw different tiles than you want and be forced to change what you're doing. Well, once you've melded a set, it's locked in for the rest of the game. Imagine you're sitting on a Bam233, and the player to your left discards a Bam4. If you call Chow, that Bam234 is now on the table and out of your hand. This means that if you draw Bam1 on your next turn, it's too late to change your mind even if Bam123 would score you more points; or if you draw Bam3, you have now lost the option of making a Pung of Bam333.

In worst-case scenarios, you may find that you've restricted yourself right out of a path to Mahjong. You might meld that Bam234 counting on making a Pure Triple Chow, but then someone else melds a Pung of Bam444 onto the table. Now that all the Bam4s are gone, you know you're never getting another Bam234 Chow, nor can you even get a Bam345 Chow for Pure Shifted Chows—and because you've melded your tiles, you can't go back and aim for Pungs instead. Melding a Chow early can be a big mistake.

On the other hand, many experts like to meld Terminal Chows (123, 789) early, and in some cases also 456. These restrict your options somewhat less than other Chows, for a few reasons. First of all, if you're holding an Edge Wait Terminal (e.g., Dot12, Crak89), it's less likely that you'd want to change your hand later, because the only thing you can really do with Dot12 aside from make Pungs is to complete it with Dot3. There are still situations where you might wish to change your mind, but they are far fewer than with regular Chows.

In addition, Terminal Chows and 456 are used in many special hands, such as Pure Straight, Mixed Straight, and the All Lowers/Middles/

Uppers hands. While melding a Bam234 would lock you out of all of these, melding a Bam123 would still leave all of those options open, as well as the more typical Mixed Triple Chows or Mixed Shifted Chows. This also has an auxiliary benefit you'll see in the next section.

Admittedly, you'll more often be eager to meld a Kong or Pung than a Chow, but there can be good reasons to hold off on those too. Obviously if an opponent's discard gives you a Kong, you want to grab it because it's your only shot. But a Kong in your hand might be something you still want to hold off on melding, if you might be able to do something useful with that fourth tile. For example, if you're holding Bam22223, you might be excited to meld the Kong of Bam2222, claiming 2 points for the Concealed Kong and drawing a replacement tile. But remember, if you can grab a Bam1 or Bam4, you might want to have the Bam222 Pung and the Bam123 or Bam234 Chow both in your hand. You'll score 2 points for Tile Hog to cover the Kong you missed out on, and, depending on the rest of your hand, you'll be in a reasonable position to go after a Half Flush or Lower Four.

Conversely, if you're looking at Honor tiles, you'll usually want to Kong because there's nothing else to do with a fourth tile. But if you're only holding a pair of Honors, it might actually be worth passing up the chance to call up a Pung from an opposing discard. Why? Well, if you have no other pairs, it can be very useful to hold on to at least one pair in your hand.

Counterintuitively, it can be easier to turn a pair into a Pung than to turn a single tile into a pair. This is because you can only call the second half of a pair from the discard if it's the last tile you need to make Mahjong, while you can call a Pung from anyone's discard at any time during the game. Also, if it's the first of that Honor to be discarded, another will likely come. If you are holding a pair of West Winds, and a third West Wind is discarded, you could call it to meld an Honor Pung.

But let's look at what happens if you let it stay discarded. With two West Winds in your hand, and a third in the discard pile, nobody else is going to use the last West Wind unless they're making a rare special hand. This means it might be discarded later, and you can always call it up as a Pung then, if you still need it. More likely, you might need to have a pair handy, and you know you won't want to break up your pair of Winds to become part of a Chow. And perhaps most importantly, if you end up not needing your pair of Winds, you can always discard them later as a very safe discard, since no other player can use them for a pair or Pung.

Discard strategies will be discussed later, but right now, it's enough to know that generally speaking, playing a meld makes your hand less flexible. But not always! If you can call up a discard to make a meld, and still leave yourself with two different ways to win, it may well be worth it. Just be aware that you are making a decision. And of course, playing your first meld also stops you from claiming the 2 points for Concealed Hand.

Melding Reveals Your Hand to Other Players

While you may not want other players to know that you are close to Mahjong when you've melded three sets, the main problem with other players seeing your hand is that it will directly affect the tiles they choose to discard. If you've melded Pungs of Dot444 and Dot555, you have basically given your opponents a big warning sign that says "Don't discard Dot3 or Dot6!" Likewise, if you meld a Chow of Dot234, the player on your left will be less likely to discard low tiles since she must suspect you are aiming for either Triple Chows or Shifted Chows.

Incidentally, this is another reason why the Terminal Chows mentioned earlier make such good early melds; they reveal almost no information. While a Dot234 may give your opponent some information about your hand, a Crak123 could be part of anything from a Mixed Straight to an All Lowers to a Shifted Chow. There is literally no suited tile in the game that cannot be part of a winning fan along with Crak123, so melding a Terminal Chow doesn't reveal much information to your opponents.

Of course, you should also be picking up information from what your opponents choose to meld. If you are trying to make any Chows in your hand, you'll want to pay special attention to what your left-hand opponent has melded. If she has melded any Bams, that increases the odds that she'll be gathering more Bams in hand, which in turn decreases the odds that she'll discard any Bams. Since you can only call discards to complete Chows from your left-hand opponent, if you think she's not going to be discarding any Bams, that's an excellent reason not to try for Chows in Bams!

Managing Your Discards

Sometimes, especially at the beginning of the game, you may find yourself with a number of tiles in your hand that aren't part of any set and don't really seem useful. How do you decide what to discard first? Well, you know you want to keep pairs, Pungs, and Chows, but with everything else, you'll have to do some prioritizing.

Usually singleton Honors will be the first tiles you want to get rid of. This can be dangerous late in the game if you might be giving someone else the second half of their Mahjong-winning pair, but early on, because they can only Pung and not Chow, Honors are less versatile when building a hand than suited tiles.

First to go should be "Off-Winds"—Winds that are neither the Prevailing nor Seat Winds. These aren't worth any extra points like the good Winds or Dragons, but also can't be part of a Chow like suit tiles. They are the worst of both worlds, and thus if you don't have a good reason to keep them, discard them immediately. Technically speaking, if one of the two Off-Winds is the Seat Wind of your left-hand opponent, you may want to discard that one. Why? Well, it's worth points to him, and if he calls up your discard to complete a Pung, as soon as he discards it, it will be your turn again, and the other two players will be skipped.

After the Off-Winds, you can discard your Seat Wind and the Prevailing Wind, and then the Dragons. If you're a few turns in, check the discard pile before discarding, as an Honor with one copy already in the discard pile is unlikely to let you complete a Pung, so it's a good candidate for discarding.

Even if they're not on the discard pile, singleton Honors in your hand are never a good thing. If you draw more it can be nice, but otherwise you'll have to discard them eventually, and this can be much more dangerous later in the game when it might hand someone a Mahjong.

Once you've tossed all your singleton Honors, next to go are the Terminals (1s and 9s). While they can be Chowed, unlike Honors, they can only be part of one specific Chow (123 or 789). They are therefore slightly less flexible than the two outer simples (2s and 8s), which can each be part of two different Chows. Once you've discarded random 2s and 8s, last to go of your unconnected tiles are 34567. These middle five tiles offer the most options for your hand, and so are the most valuable singletons to hold on to.

Of course, hopefully your hand isn't just a mishmash of unconnected tiles, but also includes a bunch of useful potential Chows. These can be triaged in a similar manner—if you are forced to discard part of a potential Chow, start by discarding tiles that rely on filling an Outside Straight (e.g., Bam568, you'd discard the 8) and edges of Terminal Chows (e.g., Dot12, you'd discard the 1 first). Pairs should be one of the last things to go, since not only are they waiting to become Pungs by calling a discard from anywhere, but you also need a pair for Mahjong! And of course, don't break up any full Chows or Pungs that you've managed to assemble.

That being said, of course any individual circumstance can be more important than a general rule. If you look at the discard pile and opposing melds and realize you can't possibly finish the Chow you were working on, it's no longer of any value to you, so it can be discarded.

Discarding Defensively

So far, most of your strategy has revolved around improving your hand. But Mahjong is a game played with three opponents, and if any one of them wins, you lose and have to pay them points. What's worse, if one of them calls Mahjong from a tile that you discarded, you'll have to pay them more points than anyone else! For this reason, much of the late-game strategy in Mahjong revolves around not discarding tiles that will hand the game to your opponents.

A hand of Mahjong is not very long. One-third of the tiles in the game start in the hands of the players. If nobody plays a Kong to grab a replacement tile, it would only take twenty-one rounds to empty the wall—and the game will usually end from a Mahjong long before that. For your first half-dozen turns or so, players probably won't be close to Mahjong, so you can worry less about discards and focus on keeping your hand flexible while you start gathering the tiles you'll need to make a Mahjong hand.

Soon, however, you'll see the number of tiles in the wall start to dwindle as only two sides of the wall remain, and the draw has gone around the table a dozen times. At this point, at least one player at the table is probably close to Mahjong. Hopefully you! If you're just waiting on one tile for Mahjong, then you can ignore all discarding strategy and just hope to draw your winning tile. If you are further away than one tile from Mahjong, however, it's time to play defensively. Defense, in Mahjong, basically means trying not to discard a tile that will hand your opponent the game.

A quick way to figure out what tiles are "safe discards" is to look at the tiles already discarded. The more copies of a tile being discarded, the safer it is for you to dispose of. The ideal discard is a tile where the total number in the discard pile and in your hand adds up to four, meaning that you know for a fact no other player is holding any of that tile. This is why you should hold on to a pair of Honors; if at the end of the game you see two West Winds in the discard pile, the two in your hand are very safe to discard, since you know nobody can make a Pung or even a pair with them (and Honors can never be in a Chow).

The more recently a player has discarded a tile, the higher the odds are that it's a safe discard. For example, a Dot2 could have been discarded on the first turn of the game, but now everyone's hands have changed and people may want one again. Whereas if your opponent discarded a Crak3 just last round and nobody called it up, Crak3 is very likely to be a safe discard.

Another thing you'll want to do is look at what tiles your opponents have melded in front of them, which will give you some idea of what types of hands they might be trying to build. As discussed earlier, some melds give you more information than others. An opponent who has melded a Pung of Dragons or a Terminal Chow isn't giving you as much information as someone who has melded two Pungs or Chows that look to be part of a shifted set. Still, even if a player's only meld is a Pung or Chow in a suit, you might guess that she would be happy to get more tiles of the same suit of around the same number.

One thing to keep in mind is that Chows can only be called from the left-hand opponent. So if you see the player across from you melding Chows of Bam234 and Bam345, you may be reasonably safe in discarding a Bam4, because he can't call it up for a Chow and not enough Bam4s remain in the game for anyone to call it up for a Pung.

Speaking of suits, if your hand consists mostly of one suit, you're probably better off holding on to that suit, if possible. This will increase your odds of putting together a special hand, whether it's a Straight, Flush, or Pure hand. Likewise, you may want to hold on to Dragons and valuable Winds. (Remember, the Prevailing Wind and your Seat Wind are worth extra points if made into a Pung.)

Another way to look into suits is to make note of the tiles that have already been discarded. If you see a lot of one suit in the discard pile, it may mean that nobody is collecting that suit. A late-game discard pile that's 80 percent Bamboo probably means that Bamboo is a safe discard. The inverse also applies: if you notice that after a number of rounds of the table, there are still almost no Dots discarded, this probably means that multiple players are collecting Dots. If you think it's late enough in the game that players might have ready hands waiting for Mahjong, you probably don't want to discard your Dots right then.

And as long as you're watching your opponent's discards, pay attention to the numbers they are discarding. You are usually safer discarding a tile that someone else has already discarded; the more copies already discarded, the safer it is to dispose. But there is an additional way to look for moderately safe discards, known as the "1-4-7 Rule."

The 1-4-7 Rule

Chows can normally only be called from the player on your left, but remember that when a tile would give you Mahjong, you may call it from anyone's discard, even if that last tile completes a Chow. For this reason, it's useful to think about how a Chow is finished. You presume that your opponents know that it is easier to fill the edge of a Chow than the middle of a Chow. You would always rather have Bam23 than Bam24, because the former gives you twice as many chances to go out. So you imagine that an opponent waiting on a Chow for Mahjong has all of his tiles in sets, aside from two adjacent numbers.

Now, let's imagine it's late in the game, and your opponent discards a Bam4. We can extrapolate that he isn't holding Bam23 as his final unfinished set, otherwise Bam4 would have completed the Chow of Bam234. And this gives you some useful information, which is that Bam1 is moderately safe since it likely won't complete a Bam123 Chow, otherwise the Bam4 would have been taken to do the same thing.

Now it's your turn, and you have to choose between discarding a Bam7 and a Dot2. Which should you discard? The Bam7 is the safer discard. If you've seen your opponent discard a Bam4, he's giving you two pieces of information: he's probably not waiting with Bam23, and he's probably not waiting with Bam56. This means whenever someone discards a 4, it means 1s and 7s in the same suit are moderately safe. And a 1 or 7 means a 4 in the same suit is moderately safe.

The same pattern holds true for 2-5-8 and 3-6-9. Of course, there are few guarantees in Mahjong, and your opponent may discard a Bam4 only to call up your Bam7 to complete a Pung of Bam777. But any information you have to improve your odds is good, and this is why the 1-4-7 Rule is frequently used when deciding what to discard.

Note that if completing the Chow would *not* give a Mahjong, it is only the player on your right who can call up your discards to make a Chow. So pay special attention to what the player on your right is discarding, and try to use the 1-4-7 Rule to avoid giving her any tiles that will help her make a Chow.

But the most important thing about discards is to be aware of when you need to start worrying about them. If you're two tiles away from Mahjong, you may want to try to stash a "safe" discard in your hand, which you can discard when the wall runs low to reduce the chances of handing your opponent the game. If the wall is running low and you are still more than three tiles away from Mahjong, it may be worth giving up on winning if this lets you discard safe tiles rather than dangerous ones. After all, while the best thing you can do is to get Mahjong, the next best thing is to avoid being the player whose discard lets someone else win!

Those are the basic strategies for International Mahjong. The only other thing to mention is the overarching strategy that will help you win more Mahjong games: play more and practice!

AMERICAN MAHJONG

While International Mahjong may be the world standard, here in the United States there is a very different variant of Mahjong that is just as popular. In this part, you will learn the rules of American Mahjong as well as some basic strategies to help you improve at the game.

CHAPTER 6

AMERICAN MAHJONG–
TILE GUIDE

The standard American Mahjong set uses 152 tiles, which includes all 144 tiles from the standard International Mahjong set. (See Chapter 2 for more in-depth background on tile meanings and a guide to interpreting Chinese characters.) Most American Mahjong sets will have Arabic numerals on the tiles, which is especially useful for distinguishing between characters. The tiles used are as follows.

Suits

There are four copies each of 1 through 9 in three suits, totaling thirty-six of each suit.

Dots

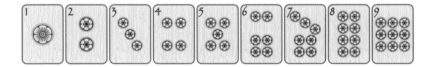

Bamboo

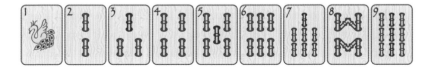

Characters

Winds

In addition to the three main suits, there are also four copies each of the four Winds. Again, American Mahjong sets tend to label these with the first English letter of the Wind direction, making it easier to distinguish between them.

Dragons

There are also four copies each of the three Dragons.

These are sometimes pictured as the exact same dragon, only replicated in different colors. More often, the White Dragon is depicted as a rectangular box or "Soap." The Soap Dragon is of particular importance in American Mahjong because it also serves as a zero—most American

Mahjong scoring cards include a few scoring hands that require tiles bearing the number of the current year, meaning that for the next eighty years or so, thanks to the combination 20XX, Soap Dragons will be especially useful.

Important to note for American Mahjong is that each Dragon has an associated suit. Red Dragons match with Craks, Green Dragons match with Bams, and the White Dragon matches with Dots. One way to remember this is by color: in most sets, the Craks are Red and the Bams are Green. Conversely, you can try to remember that Bamboo is green and the Soap Dragon is like a rectangular dot. If all else fails, the scorecard will remind you which Dragon goes with which suit. This will matter when putting together your hand.

Bonus Tiles (Flowers and Seasons)

There are eight bonus tiles, each with an individual picture.

American Mahjong sets often put the first three letters of the season on each Season tile (SPR, SUM, AUT, WIN, for 1, 2, 3, 4). In American Mahjong sets, it is especially important not to confuse the 1 of Flower (Plum) with the 1 of Bamboo (Bird), since both have a number 1. Although there are four Flowers and four Seasons, all eight tiles are simply treated as Flowers for the purposes of American Mahjong.

Joker Tiles

Finally, there are eight Joker tiles. These are all identical, and generally say "Joker" right on them. They can be used as wildcards—but only for sets of three of a kind or more. Jokers can also never be called from the discard.

Non-Tile Components

Also in your American Mahjong set, you will find a pair of standard six-sided dice, rolled to determine the dealer and the break point in the wall. Some sets also include a dealer marker (that sits in front of the dealer so players recall who dealt the hand), which sometimes includes a Prevailing Wind marker (to track the round).

Racks are often used to hold your tiles, making it easier to arrange your hand without accidentally flipping over a tile. Some racks are equipped with pusher arms, used to help form the wall. Many players use chips or scoring sticks instead of money, in which case each player must start with an equal value of chips. This can range from 500 to 20,000, depending on the table.

CHAPTER 7

AMERICAN MAHJONG– SETUP

Before you can jump into the action of a game and start drawing and discarding tiles, the game must be properly set up. A dealer must be chosen, a wall formed, and opening hands distributed. Only then can a game of American Mahjong begin with the Charleston.

Picking the Dealer

Before you can start the game, the first thing you must do is select a dealer. Usually you will do this by having each player roll two dice. The highest roll becomes East, and will deal the first hand. The player with the next-highest total sits to their right and becomes South, the next-highest total across from East becomes West, and the player with the lowest total sits to the left of East and becomes North.

If you are already sitting and do not wish to get up, you may assign the highest roller as East, and then declare the player to their right as South, followed by West and North. Or, if you are playing a casual game with friends, you can skip the dice-off entirely and simply assign the host/hostess as East.

Creating the Wall

All 152 tiles are placed facedown in the middle of the table, and then all players help to mix them up thoroughly with both hands. As the tiles are being mixed, try to keep them facedown as much as possible. If some tiles end up getting flipped face-up, simply flip them facedown and continue mixing. Once the tiles are all thoroughly mixed, each player takes facedown tiles and builds a wall in front of him or herself, often using their tile rack or "pusher" as a flat edge for squaring the tiles. The wall should be two tiles high, and nineteen tiles long.

Once all of the players have built their walls, the four walls are pushed toward the center of the table in a square with open corners, making them easier for all players to reach. The active wall is often pushed in diagonally to make it especially easy to reach; many players will use their tile racks, or pusher bars, to do this.

Distributing the Tiles

The dealer (East) rolls two dice to determine the break point in the wall. First, the dice are thrown to determine who has the starting wall. The dealer counts counterclockwise, with the dealer's own wall (East) counting as 1, South as 2, West as 3, North as 4, East again as 5, and so on, until the appropriate number is reached (i.e., if the dice roll a 7, West will be the starting wall). In some variants or casual play, this step is skipped, and East is always the starting wall.

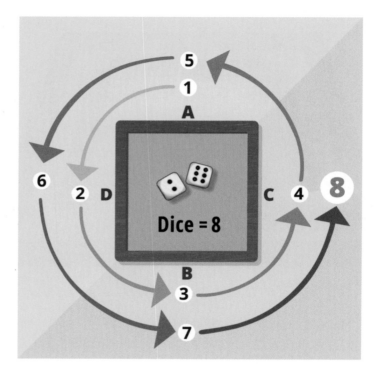

Once a starting wall has been chosen, it is time to choose a break point. First, the player who has the starting wall pushes their tile line so the right edge approaches the center, making a more diagonal wall, in order to make it easier for all players to reach. Using the number rolled on the dice in the previous paragraph to choose a starting wall (or throwing the dice now if that step was skipped), the player on the starting wall counts that many tiles from the right edge of her wall, and separates the wall at that point to make a break. The line of tiles to the right of the break point is now pushed back against the rack and pusher, so only half the diagonal line remains.

With a break in the wall now accomplished, East then takes the first two stacks (four tiles) from the left of the break point. South takes the next four tiles, West the next four, and North the next four. This is repeated twice more around the table, so each player has twelve tiles.

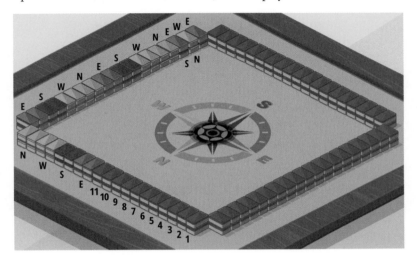

The final tiles are taken in a different way. East takes the first and third available top tiles, leaving a pattern that looks a bit like a crenellated castle wall. South then takes the first revealed bottom tile, West takes the next top tile, and North takes the next (newly revealed) bottom tile.

With the tiles now dealt, it's time to choose a hand! Chapter 11 goes into more detail about gameplay strategy, but for now, just pick something on your scorecard that matches as many tiles as possible. Once you have an idea of what you're doing, you're ready for the first choice of the game, unique to American Mahjong: the Charleston.

CHAPTER 8

AMERICAN MAHJONG– THE CHARLESTON

Named after the popular dance that swept the country in the 1920s at the same time as Mahjong, the Charleston is a "dance of tiles," in which players will pass tiles to one another. The most important rule of the Charleston is this: *no Jokers may be passed* during the Charleston at any point.

First Charleston

The "First Charleston" describes the first three passes, all of which are mandatory. These passes are:

1. **First Right:** Each player *must* pass three tiles facedown to the player on their right. This is done simultaneously, so you must choose which of your tiles to pass before picking up the tiles passed to you.
2. **First Across:** Each player *must* pass exactly three tiles facedown to the player sitting directly across from them. This is all done simultaneously, so you must choose which three of your tiles to pass before picking up the tiles being passed to you.
3. **First Left:** Here is where it gets a little interesting. Each player must pass three tiles to their left. However, in this third pass if you do not want to remove three tiles from your hand, you are allowed to make what is known as an optional Blind Pass. You may take any number of the three tiles you are receiving from your right, and without looking at them, pass them along facedown to your left as part of the three tiles you must pass. This is also known as "stealing" some tiles to pass.

For example, imagine that after the First Right and First Across, your hand consists mostly of pairs and triplets, with only a single Bam1 standing alone that doesn't fit any hands you are aiming for. You might opt to pass only the Bam1 from your hand, along with taking two of the tiles being passed to you without looking at them, for a total of the three tiles that you must pass. You would then pick up the third tile being passed to you, the only one you did not steal for a Blind Pass, and add that last tile to your hand to replace the one tile from your hand that you passed.

Those three passes make up the First Charleston. Once the First Charleston is complete, there may be a Second Charleston by unanimous agreement of the players. If even a single player says, "No thanks, no more Charlestons for me" (presumably because they have a good hand they do not wish to break up by being forced to pass three tiles), the Second Charleston is skipped.

Second Charleston

The steps to the Second Charleston are:

1. **Second Left:** Each player *must* pass exactly three tiles facedown to the player on their left. This is all done simultaneously, so you must choose which three of your tiles to pass before picking up the tiles being passed to you. (Note that the exchange is done in the opposite direction from the start of the First Charleston.)
2. **Second Across:** Each player *must* simultaneously pass exactly three tiles facedown to the player sitting directly across from them.
3. **Final Right:** So named because it is always the final step of the Charlestons, this final pass is another chance to hold on to more tiles if you don't wish to give up three. Each player must pass three tiles facedown to their right, but it is another optional Blind Pass, meaning that one, two, or even all three of those tiles may be taken from the incoming tiles (without looking) rather than off your rack.

After the Final Right (or, if the Second Charleston has been canceled, after the First Left), the Charleston is over, but there is one more chance to improve your hand: the Courtesy Pass.

The Courtesy Pass

Each player may, by mutual agreement with the player directly across from them, exchange up to three tiles facedown. Agreement always tends to the lowest number. In other words, if North wishes to exchange three tiles, and South only wishes to exchange two, North and South exchange two tiles. If any player wishes to exchange zero tiles, the player across from them is out of luck because those two players won't exchange tiles. It is quite possible that the two pairs of players at the table will exchange different numbers of tiles.

Summing Up the Charleston

In summary, the passing of the Charleston looks like this:

1. First Charleston
   - First Right
   - First Across
   - First Left (Optional Blind Pass)
2. (If All Agree) Second Charleston
   - Second Left
   - Second Across
   - Final Right (Optional Blind Pass)
3. Courtesy Pass

Just keep that order in mind, and remember, passing Jokers is not allowed.

CHAPTER 9

AMERICAN MAHJONG– RULES

After the Charleston, the real action of the game begins. You'll be drawing and discarding tiles, as well as potentially calling up the discarded tiles of other players. And if you're lucky, you may even be able to redeem one of your tiles for an opponent's Joker. When the hand ends, the winning player will have a set of tiles that specifically matches one of the combinations listed on the scorecard.

Starting the Round

With the players seated, the wall built, the opening hands taken, and the Charleston complete, it's finally time to start the game! Your goal in the game is to create a Mahjong, which is a hand that exactly matches one of the hands on your scorecard.

It is technically possible that after the Charleston, the East player will start the game by declaring a Mahjong. This is incredibly rare, but in the unlikely event it happens, East simply reveals their hand and claims Mahjong. Chances are, you will never see this happen, in which case East starts the hand by discarding a tile.

Whenever a tile is discarded, all players have a few seconds to claim it before the next player starts their turn. If no one does, the turn passes counterclockwise around the table, which means after East, the South player (on East's right) would take the next turn.

On Your Turn

When it is your turn, here are the steps to follow:

1. **Wait.** Allow a few seconds to see if anyone (possibly including you!) wants to claim the most recently discarded tile. If so, skip the rest of this section and move to "Claiming the Discard."
2. **Draw the next tile from the wall.** The next tile will always be clockwise from the break point. If there is a single bottom tile with nothing stacked atop it, that's the next tile. If not, take the top tile from the next stack.
3. **Is it Mahjong?** See if your hand is now a valid Mahjong, exactly matching one of the hands on the scorecard. Be sure to remember that hands with a C next to them are Concealed and cannot be completed if you have any exposed tiles from calling a discard. If you can match a hand on the scorecard, you declare Mahjong and win the round! Skip ahead to "Declaring Mahjong." Otherwise, move on to Step 4.
4. **Exchanging for exposed Jokers.** On your turn after drawing your tile, if any exposure contains a Joker, you may swap a tile in your hand for that Joker if it matches the exposure (i.e., an opponent has an exposed Kong of Dot6, Dot6, Joker, Dot6; you may take a Dot6 from your hand and exchange it with the Joker). This is sometimes known as "redeeming" a tile, and does not end your turn.
5. **Discard a tile.** Pick a tile from your hand that you no longer want, and place it face-up in the middle of the table. When you discard a tile, you must announce the name of the tile (i.e., "Bam1" or "Red Dragon"). Once you have discarded a tile, your turn is over. The turn will then pass to the next player on your right, unless someone claims the discard. (Jokers are special when it comes to discarding: when you discard a Joker, you may say "Joker," or you may instead say "Same," or the name of the tile that was discarded just prior.)

Claiming the Discard

Whenever a tile is discarded, before the next player starts his turn, there is a short window of a few seconds when any player may "Call" to lay claim to the most recently discarded tile, which lasts until the active player has drawn his tile from the wall and either racked it into his hand or discarded it onto the table. If playing with any new players, it is recommended that this window of opportunity last a little longer. Experienced players will likely shorten this window.

Note that unless you are playing with a specialized variant, a Joker can never be called from the discard for any reason. Any other tile, immediately after being discarded, may be called up for one of two reasons.

Mahjong

Any player may call Mahjong and claim the most recently discarded tile as his fourteenth and final tile to form Mahjong. A player claiming a tile to make Mahjong has priority over all exposure claims. If multiple players claim the same tile for Mahjong, priority goes to the player whose turn was coming soonest, i.e., highest priority to the right of the discarding player. (Note that in some variants, single tiles may never be called from the discard, even to complete a Mahjong. Only pairs or more of a kind may be called from the discard to complete a Mahjong, meaning that if the final tile you need is a singleton, you must draw it from the wall.)

In the case of a tile being claimed for Mahjong, the round is ended, and the claiming player is the winner. Skip the rest of this section, and see the next section under "Declaring Mahjong" for more information on what to do next.

Exposure

If no player is calling the most recently discarded tile for Mahjong, any player may claim that tile if it will complete a Pung (three identical tiles), a Kong (four identical tiles), a Quint (five identical tiles), or a

Sextet (six identical tiles). The calling player says "Call" to take the tile. If multiple players claim the same tile for an exposure, priority goes to the player whose turn was coming soonest—i.e., highest priority to the right of the discarding player.

Once you successfully call up a tile for an exposure, you must immediately create the exposure. Take the called-up tile, along with the proper number of matching tiles from your hand, and place them all face-up in front of you.

Note that once melded, an exposure may never be modified. This means that you cannot change your mind and add another tile to transform a Pung into a Kong for a different hand, nor may you subtract a tile to turn a Kong into a Pung, nor may you pick up the tiles for a Concealed Hand. After you play an exposure, you are committed to a Mahjong hand that uses that exact set!

Once a player has called up a tile and made an exposure, that player then discards a tile as if it were the end of her turn, and play continues to her right.

Declaring Mahjong

A Mahjong is a hand that exactly matches one of the hands of fourteen tiles on the scorecard. If you have a matching hand, you may declare Mahjong, but before you do, be sure that you aren't making one of these common mistakes:

- If the hand on the card says "C" or "Concealed," you cannot declare Mahjong if you have any exposures.
- If the hand requires any singletons or pairs, you cannot use a Joker as part of those sets. Jokers are only used for three or more of a kind. (A "Year" set such as "2018" is considered four singletons. So if your hand required "2018 FFFF NEWS," you could use a Joker as a Flower for the Kong, but not for the Year or for the singleton Winds.)

- Be sure you have read the suits required for your chosen hand on the scorecard correctly. Some of your sets may have to be the same or different suits as others—and in those cases, the suits of Dragons can matter!

If you're sure that you're not making any of these common mistakes, go ahead and declare Mahjong!—but be careful. If you declare Mahjong and reveal your hand does not match correctly with the hand on the scorecard, your hand is declared a Dead Hand—you drop out of the hand and take no further turns, your hand is revealed, and you are forced to pay the true winner at the end of the round.

If you declare Mahjong and reveal a legal scoring hand, congratulations! It's time to rake in your profits!

Scoring the Hand

The scorecard will tell you the base value of the hand, and then all other players must pay the winner that value multiplied by two adjustments:

1. If the Mahjong is made by calling a discard, the discarding player pays the winner double the hand value, and the two other players pay the single value. If the Mahjong is completed by picking a tile off the wall, all three players pay the winner double value.
2. If the winning hand *could* use Jokers, but contains no Jokers, all payments are doubled. (This does not apply to singleton and pair hands, such as NEWS 2018, which can never use Jokers. But it does apply to hands filled with 3333 FFFF DDDD 6666, if Jokers would be allowed, but were not used.) This doubling of payment stacks with the doubling in the previous adjustment, so a lucky winner could end up getting four times the base-hand value!

Here is an example: you call a discard to achieve a Joker-less Mahjong (on a hand that could use Jokers). The hand value is $0.25. The discarding player must pay you double for discarding, doubled again for Joker-less, making a total of $1. The other two players must pay you only the base rate for not discarding, but then doubled for Joker-less, for a total of $0.50 each. This means your take on the hand would be $1 + $0.50 + $0.50 = $2, which is pretty good for a $0.25 hand!

Although rare, it is possible that the last tile will be pulled from the wall without any player achieving Mahjong. If this happens, it is considered a Wall Game (or Draw), and no payments are made.

Either way, after the hand ends, all tiles are pushed into the center and mixed up again, and the dealer position (and the title of "East") passes right to the next player.

CHAPTER 10

AMERICAN MAHJONG– READING THE SCORECARD

In order to choose the hand you'll be aiming for, you'll want to consult your scorecard. Most players playing American Mahjong use an official National Mah Jongg League (NMJL) scorecard, which is a list of legal hands that changes every year. You could certainly order the current one for yourself by going to NationalMahJonggLeague.org, but you could just as easily search up an older card from a previous year, or even make up your own scorecard following the NMJL style. The most important thing is that everyone at your table is reading the same scorecard, and that you understand how to read it.

Categories

The first thing you'll notice is that the scorecard is broken up into categories, each of which contain hands that use similar elements. Some categories you might see include:

- **Year Hands.** Hands that contain singletons of the current year (i.e., 2018), using a White Dragon as zero. These generally (but not always) require a lot of Honor tiles.
- **369, 13579, 2468.** Hands that require multiple copies of the specific numbers stated in that category.
- **Like Numbers, Quints.** Hands that require many copies of a number, but generally (although not always) any number can be used.

- **Winds-Dragons.** Hands using many copies of Honor tiles (Winds and Dragons).
- **Consecutive Runs.** Hands that require multiple copies of numbers in a row, but usually not any specific number.
- **Addition Hands, Multiplication Hands.** Hands that require many copies of specific numbers, listed in a mathematical formula (e.g., FF 4444 + 5555 = 9999: this hand would require three Kongs of those specific numbers and a pair of Flowers).
- **Singles and Pairs.** Hands that do not use any Pungs, Kongs, and so on, but consist entirely of single tiles and pairs. Note that because the hand contains no Pungs, these hands are always concealed (can never be called from the discard) and contain no Jokers.

Within each category, you will see a list of hands. A hand consists of a set of numbers and letters in up to three colors, often followed by a parenthetical explanation, and always followed by a point value and either an X or a C. Let's break down how to read a hand.

Decoding the Hands

Here are all the abbreviations you'll need to know:

- N: North Wind
- E: East Wind
- W: West Wind
- S: South Wind
- F: Flower (any)
- D: Dragon
- 1–9: Tiles of appropriate number
- 0: White Dragon

- X: Does not appear in hand, but in front of the point value. Stands for Exposed Hand, which means you can call discarded tiles and meld exposures to help you win the hand.
- C: Does not appear in hand, but in front of the point value. Stands for Concealed Hand, which means you cannot have any exposures, and therefore cannot have called for discarded tiles before the last tile of the game.
- Point value: Base amount you will get paid from each player if you win with the indicated hand. Note that this amount will always be doubled at least once by at least one opponent, so even a lowly 25 points (the lowest-valued hand on most scorecards) will be guaranteed to fetch you no less than 100 points, and often more.

Colors

The last thing you need to know to decode the scorecard is that it is generally printed in three colors. The number of colors used in listing a hand tells you how many suits the hand will require. Each color in the hand can be any suit you like, but must be consistent throughout the hand. This means if you have 222 444 666 888 DD, all in blue, that means you must use only a single suit to have 222, 444, 666, 888, and DD.

Remember that Dragons each match a suit—Green Dragons with Bams (which are also green), Red Dragons with Craks (which are also red), and White Dragons with Dots. So in that example hand, if you had your four Pungs of Crak2, Crak4, Crak6, and Crak8, you would need a pair of Red Dragons to finish the hand. If you had a pair of Green Dragons instead, you'd need the rest of your hand to be Bam.

When two colors are used in the hand, it works the same way. You can think of it as two smaller hands intertwined, one of each color, because all the numbers and letters in red must be of one suit, and all the numbers and letters in green must be of a second, different suit.

Remember, Flowers, Winds, and zeros do not have any particular suit, and will always be listed in blue/standard font. If a Dragon needs to match colors, it will be listed as a D. If it's listed as a zero, it has to be a White Dragon, but that White Dragon has no suit.

The final wrinkle, of course, is that the parenthetical notes have the highest priority in analyzing a hand. Sometimes these will just be to clarify; i.e., with an all-blue hand of NNN EE WW SSS 2018, there might be a parenthetical note saying (any 2, 1, and 8, same suit), to remind you that neither the Winds nor the zero as Soap Dragon force you into a particular suit.

But sometimes these parenthetical notes are important. Especially in hands of like numbers and consecutives, they will sometimes say, "Any like numbers." This lets you know that although the hand may show FFFF DDDD 111 111, you could complete it just as well with 222 222 or 777 777.

Likewise, if a parenthetical note says, "Any three consecutive numbers," then you can play your 555 666 777 even if the scorecard shows 111 222 333. Some parenthetical instructions may be more specific to the particular hand or year—just follow whatever they say!

CHAPTER 11

AMERICAN MAHJONG– STRATEGY

Though it may use many of the same tiles and rules as International Mahjong, the strategy in American Mahjong is somewhat different, owing largely to the fact that there are very specific hands that players are aiming for. To succeed at American Mahjong, you'll not only need to know what to pass in the Charleston and what hands to target, but also how to consider the target hands of your opponents.

Choosing a Hand

You've sat down and chosen a dealer, the tiles have been shuffled, the wall has been built, and you have received a hand of tiles. Now it's time to make your first, and possibly most important, decision of the game: what hand are you going to aim for?

While most other variations of Mahjong allow for varying degrees of flexibility to win with whatever applicable sets you manage to put together, American Mahjong requires you to exactly match a specific hand from a list of sequences on a scoring card. In other words, you can't just hope to draw into workable sets; you'll need to plan out your specific winning hand ahead of time.

Arranging Your Hand

The first thing you'll want to do is arrange your hand. This will make it much easier for you to analyze your tiles and figure out the best thing to do with them. Most players prefer to organize their hand by suits first, and then numbers ascending within the suit. In other words, you could put all your Flowers on the left, followed by Bams, then Dots, then Craks, then Winds, then Dragons, and finally Jokers.

Here's a sample hand you might be dealt if you are East (thus fourteen tiles), arranged by suit (see **HAND 11.1**).

You aren't required to arrange your hand this way; it's just the most traditional arrangement because it makes it easy to compare your hand to the scorecard. For American Mahjong you might consider arranging your hand as if Dragons were actually 10s in their respective suits (remember, Red Dragons go with Craks, Green Dragons with Bams, and White Dragons with Dots). Rather than keeping the Dragons separate with the Winds, this puts them with their matching suits—important because most of the winning hands that use Dragons will require them to be matched to the suit of the numbers (see **HAND 11.2**).

When comparing your hand to the scorecard, it's nice to be able to see if a hand requires 2222 DDD in one color and 8888 DDD in another color; this way you can more easily assess how close you are to matching

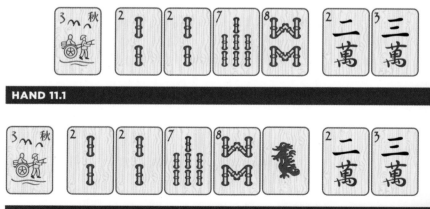

HAND 11.1

HAND 11.2

PART 3. AMERICAN MAHJONG

the required numbers with the required Dragons. But of course it's entirely up to you. You can group Dragons with suits, or you can use the traditional method of putting the Dragons on the end, or you can even invent your own method that puts Dragons in the middle.

The one thing you don't want to do is separate your tiles on your rack into groups based on like tiles or some such quality. It may be tempting to "sort" your hand by keeping your pairs and Pungs as separate groups of two and three tiles, but the backs of your tiles still peek over the edge of your rack, and your opponents can gain too much information if you do this.

Finding Your Category

Once you've arranged your hand, it's time to select a category. Scorecards in American Mahjong are grouped into nine to twelve different general categories of hand, each of which has a short list of valid hands in that category. Because categories are labeled based on their most prominent feature, it shouldn't be too difficult to compare your hand with the

various categories on the card and see which categories you have the most tiles for.

As you may recall from the previous chapter, categories include:

- **369, 13579, 2468**—use multiple copies of the numbers in category title
- **Consecutive Runs**—use multiple copies of numbers in a row, have many options
- **Year Hands**—use tiles of the current year, e.g., 2018, and often lots of Honors
- **Like Numbers, Quints**—use many copies of a number
- **Winds and Dragons**—use many Winds and Dragons
- **Addition, Multiplication**—use many copies of specific numbers (i.e., 44 + 55 = 99)
- **Singles and Pairs**—use only singles and pairs, no Jokers allowed

Because the hands in each category share tiles in common, at the beginning of the game it is generally best to pick one category that you have many tiles for, and ideally be able to make progress toward multiple hands in that category at once. If you're not familiar with the scorecard, this can seem overwhelming at first, but once you figure out how to read the card it's not too difficult. (For this reason, if you will be playing a lot, time spent familiarizing yourself with the scorecard to the point where you know some of the winning hands by heart is never wasted!) A sample scorecard by category is on the opposite page.

How Do You Choose a Category?

The scoring cards are conveniently sorted into categories, and so your first job at the beginning of the game is to figure out two things:

1. Which categories do you have the most tiles for?
2. Which categories do you have the most pairs for?

2018 (YEAR HANDS)

NNN EE WW SSS 2018

NNN 2018 2018 DDD

2468

22 444 44 666 66 88

222 444 66 DD DD DD

ADDITION HANDS

2222 + 2222 = 4444 DD

4444 + 4444 = 8888 FF

QUINTS

22222 3333 444 55 (any four consecutive numbers)

66666 DD 99999 DD (these numbers only)

CONSECUTIVE RUNS

111 222 333 DDD FF (any three consecutive numbers)

111 2222 333 4444 (any four consecutive numbers)

13579

111 333 555 777 99

11 33 333 55 77 999

WINDS AND DRAGONS

FF NNN EEE WWW SSS

NNN SS DDD DDD DDD

SINGLES AND PAIRS

11 22 33 44 55 66 77 (any seven consecutive numbers)

NEWS 2018 2018 DD

It's important to consider pairs (or if you're lucky, Pungs or Kongs), and not just single tiles, because getting multiple of a kind is required for almost every winning hand in the game, and consequently you're likely going to want a starting point to build from. When it comes to choosing a category, the number of your pairs or triplets you can use is almost as important as the raw number of tiles you have that will fit that category.

Rather than counting for each individual category, a quick type analysis of your hand will tell you which categories you ought to be checking. Let's do a quick checklist rundown:

- **Do you have many Jokers?** If you have a lot of Jokers, the Quints and Like Numbers sections are worth a good look, since they often require many of the same number, but allow flexibility as to which number, making them perfect for a hand with a few Jokers. Conversely, if you have zero Jokers, it's worth taking a quick look at the Singles and Pairs section, since no Jokers can be used there anyway.
- **Do you have a lot of Winds and Dragons?** If so, chances are that you should be looking in the Winds and Dragons section.
- **Do you have mostly suited numbers?** In most cases, the answer to this question will be yes! That's because most of the tiles in the game fall into this category. If you have a few pairs or triplets it can be worth a quick peek at the math categories, but mostly you'll be looking at more-general number trends.
- **Do you have mostly high or low (or middle) numbers?** If so, you might consider aiming for the Consecutive Run category.

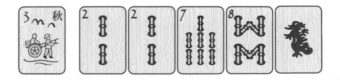

HAND 11.2

- **Do you have lots of 3s, 6s, and 9s?** If so, the 369 category is probably the place to look.
- **Do you have a lot more even numbers or odd numbers?** There's an even category for 2468, and an odd category for 13579, so if your hand is lopsided in either direction, these can be useful categories to consider. The average hand will lean slightly odd, because there are twelve more odd tiles in the game than even.

Fitting Your Tiles Into a Category

Once you've figured out which categories *might* be good fits, it's time to count up the number of tiles you have that might fit each category. Let's take a look at the example hand again (see **HAND 11.2**).

What leaps out at you? You have only a single Joker, which doesn't really push you toward Quints or Pairs. You have only two Dragons, hardly enough for a Dragon and Wind hand. Your hand is, as usual, mostly numbers. You've only got three tiles toward 369 (Crak336), so that's probably a bad choice. And you have fewer odd numbers than average.

What you do have is a fair bunch of even numbers, and two pairs of Bam22 and Crak33. So the most fruitful categories for you to look at are 2468 for evens, and Consecutive Runs for your low numbers. Tallying up your tiles, you end up with six even numbers, and also six numbers that fall between 2 and 5. In addition, your two Dragons and single Flower might also find a home in either of those two categories. (Jokers,

of course, will be a help in any category aside from Singles and Pairs.) Your pair of Bam22 can find a home easily in either category, while your Crak33 can only work in the Consecutive Run category. This may lean you slightly toward the latter, but you can't know for sure until you drill down to specific hands.

At this point, you know you want to aim for one of those two categories. To figure out which, you probably need to delve into the hands themselves. So, looking at the scorecard, you'll try to find hands that make use of your pairs at the same time as other tiles in your hand. It's unlikely that you can use every tile you have that fits your best category at once in a single hand. (If you could, you'd immediately target that hand!)

Instead, you'll likely find that only certain tiles can be used together. You prioritize the use of your pairs, since you'll need multiples of tiles and it would be a shame to not use the few you already have! In the 2468 section, you know that Bam22 can be used in pretty much any hand. But how many other tiles can you squeeze in at once? From our sample scorecard, neither hand lets you use your Bam8 along with your Bam22. The first hand lets you use Bam22, Crak6, Dot8, or the second hand lets you use Bam22, G, R. Either of these lets you use four tiles.

Now let's examine Consecutive Runs. You have two possible pairs here. And the second hand in the category will even let you use both pairs together, Bam22 Crak33, although it eliminates your other tiles that fit the category. Likewise, you could make a hand with Crak233, R, F, which drops one of your pairs, but uses five tiles instead of four.

At this point, between the ability to use pairs and the ability to use more tiles, you should probably lean toward picking Consecutive Run as your target category. Again, this is not atypical; due to its flexibility, Consecutive Run will often be one of your better options if you are not dealt all evens/odds/Honors. And within the Consecutive Run category, there is often a hand on the scorecard that uses any four consecutive numbers split among two suits, and requires no pairs (meaning you can use Jokers and/or call discards), making this a fine hand to target.

There are a few other points you may wish to factor in when considering the difficulty of achieving hands:

1. **The mathematical odds of drawing the tiles you need.** If you are aiming for a 22 444 666 88 NEWS hand, that can be achieved in any suit. You might claim Mahjong with a trio of Bam2s, or a trio of Dot2s, or a trio of Crak2s. In other words, there are a dozen 2s that started in the wall, and you only need three of them to win.

   Now let's compare that to a sequence of DD NNN EEE WWW SSS. If you are holding a bunch of odd numbers and NEWS, you might think you are equally close to completing either sequence, since you have the same number of tiles toward each. But while there are a dozen 2s, 4s, 6s, and 8s in a Mahjong set, there are only four of each Wind. For this reason, sequences that require a specific Wind are generally more difficult than sequences only requiring numbers of any suit. Math also comes into play in the combinations of numbers, not just the individual tiles. It may be easier to draw 234 of a suit than a trio of 4s, but it's going to be much harder to draw 123456789 of a single suit than a few trios across suits—especially if you're playing with Jokers.

2. **The odds of your opponent discarding the tiles you need.** You may notice that Flowers are used in a wide variety of scoring hands, and may be used with any suit. For this reason, players are unlikely to discard Flowers very often, which means that aiming for a hand that requires FF if you are not starting with any Flowers can be somewhat risky.

3. **Certain hands that have a C next to their point value (instead of an X) are concealed.** A Concealed Hand means that you may not take any discards to add to your hand, unless it is the final tile to give you Mahjong. This means that if another player discards a tile you need, you may be out of luck as it is now out of the game forever and you have no way to get it.

All that being said, your primary consideration when evaluating categories and hands is always going to be how many of your tiles you can use. Regardless, once you've selected your category, you know what tiles you need to keep, and can also figure out what tiles to pass. Which means it's time for the Charleston.

The Charleston

The Charleston represents an opportunity for you to refine your hand and get it closer to a winning combination. You generally don't want to give away anything from your chosen category, but if you have lots of tiles you don't need and are looking for an excuse to keep some, you can also hold on to tiles from the other category you almost chose, for now. You can think of the following as a priority hold list, in order of what's most important to keep:

- **0) Jokers.** Jokers are not allowed to be passed in the Charleston. (And even if they were, you probably wouldn't want to, because they're very useful.)
- **1) Tiles for your chosen category/hands.** Obviously, in order to win, the most important thing is to hold on to the tiles you'll need for your winning hands! Once you finish a few passes of the Charleston, you'll switch over to only holding tiles for the hands you are closest to. But at the beginning of the game, you should have plenty of tiles that don't match your category at all, so pass those first! (If you don't have three tiles outside of your category, you have a pretty good opening hand!)
- **2) Flowers.** As mentioned, Flowers are required for a number of winning hands, there are only eight of them in the game, and because they do not have a suit, they are easy to use no matter what suit the rest of your hand is. For this reason, it's worth holding on to them in the Charleston even if you don't think you'll need them, because your opponents will probably want them, and you would prefer your opponents to lose.

- **3) Pairs.** Even if you're not using them in your category at the moment, a pair is always potentially useful, and there's always the chance that you'll be passed enough to make use of it later.
- **4) Honors.** All else being equal, Honor tiles (Winds and Dragons) are required for a number of the winning hands, and consequently these tiles may be in shorter supply.
- **5) Anything else.** Tiles that don't fall in any of the previous categories are completely pointless for you, and can be passed with impunity.

This checklist outlines what tiles you want to hold on to (and avoid passing to your opponents). As previously discussed, you should rarely pass an opponent Flowers, but also never pass an opponent a full pair. If you have a pair in your hand that you no longer need and want to get rid of, try to pass half to one opponent and half to a different opponent. Let's go back to the example hand (see **HAND 11.2**).

You aren't allowed to pass the Joker, you want to hold FGR for now, and you need Bam22, Crak233, Dot5 for your category. This leaves you with Bam78, Crak6, Dot8 as the four tiles you're happiest to get rid of. But what will your opponents receive? You want to pay attention and avoid passing your opponent three tiles in the same category—in this case, the tiles you want to get rid of could all be used in a high Consecutive Run, and all but the 7 could also be used in the 2468 category. That's fine; you're not passing any pairs or Flowers, so we're not too concerned about tiles that could be in one category, although you'll probably want to hold the Bam8 to give away on your second pass, just to minimize the help your right-hand opponent is getting. You can pass Bam7, Crak6, Dot8 for the First Right, and probably not worry too much about it.

However, you will want to make a mental note of the fact that you're passing tiles for a certain category to the right. If you're serious about the game, you might watch your opponent and try to see if the tiles you pass her get placed on her rack, or if she just passes them across on the next pass. If she keeps the tiles, or you can't tell, you should probably try not to pass her more 678 tiles in the Second Charleston, just to be safe.

Meanwhile, you were handed three new tiles to replace the three you passed. You receive Dot79 and G, so your hand is now the following (see **HAND 11.3**).

If you have a good memory, you can try to return what players pass you later in the Charleston. Here, your left-hand neighbor has handed you odd high Dots, which means, if possible, you can prioritize returning them the same, or at the very least you should avoid handing them low even Bams and Craks if you have the flexibility to do so. Obviously as you approach better hands you may only have a few tiles to pass, but as long as you have the option, you may as well make things more difficult for your opponents!

Your returns here aren't great. You picked up a second Green Dragon, giving you a pair that could be useful if you go for your alternate Consecutive Run hand. Even if you were sticking with your favored hand, you certainly wouldn't want to pass them both to the same player. Beyond that, unless you're out of options for tiles to pass, you'd prefer to hold on

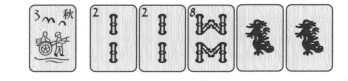

HAND 11.3

HAND 11.4

to a pair even if you're not using it. There are advantages to having a pair in hand that you want to discard, as will be discussed.

Meanwhile, it's time to pass your First Across, and in the absence of anything better, you're passing Bam8, Dot79 to your opponent across. Let's see what he hands you back: Bam19, Crak4. Let's check your hand again (see **HAND 11.4**).

That's more like it! The Bam1 goes nicely with your pair of Bam2s, just as the Crak4 goes nicely with your pair of Crak3s. Checking your scorecard again, you now have seven tiles toward the second Consecutive Run hand (Bam122, Crak334, J), as well as toward the two-number Consecutive Run hand (F, Bam122, GG, J). Once you hit the seven-tile threshold on multiple hands, you can start worrying less about the category and more about the tiles that will benefit those two hands.

Tiles you're currently not using for either hand are: Bam9, Crak2, R, Dot5. Note that if you only had one or two tiles you weren't using for either hand, First Left is your chance to do a Blind Pass and steal some tiles to pass along without changing your hand as much. But you have more than three useless tiles, so you'd like to change your hand! Let's

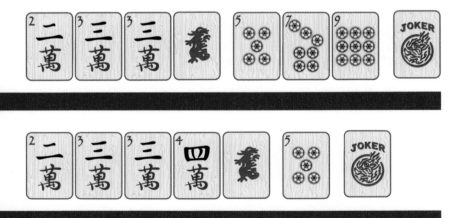

hold the Dragon and pass the rest for First Left. Your right-hand neighbor gives you Bam17, Crak5. That leaves your hand at the following (see **HAND 11.5**).

You're pretty happy with another Bam1, putting you only six tiles away from a Mahjong at the end of the First Charleston if you make your formerly secondary hand into a primary hand and vice versa. You still have three tiles you don't need for either of your target hands (Bam7, Crak5, R), so you'd be perfectly happy to do a Second Charleston as long as nobody else at the table objects. Looking back at the First Charleston, you see that you received seven odd numbers, and only a single Honor and even tile, so people may be holding on to Honors and evens.

If everyone had agreed to a Second Charleston, you'd do another round of three passes, this time starting on the left. But in this case, imagine one player vetoed the Second Charleston. The two main reasons to veto a Second Charleston are if you are fairly close to Mahjong, or if you are aiming for an Exposed Hand with many Pungs, and have a lot of pairs that you want to call up discards for to complete. Either way, if any opponent vetoes the Second Charleston, the exchange doesn't occur.

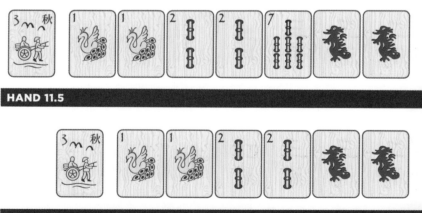

HAND 11.5

HAND 11.6

Instead, you get one final opportunity for a Courtesy Pass. (Note that if the Second Charleston had happened, the Courtesy Pass would follow.)

You have plenty of unwanted tiles, so you ask to pass three tiles with your opponent across. (Note that if he was the one who stopped the Charleston, he is probably close to Mahjong, so you would want to be especially careful with what you passed him, keeping in mind both what you received from him and what you gave him previously.) He only wants to pass two tiles, and since the rules state that the lower number chosen by the two opposed players is what happens, you'll exchange two tiles for the Courtesy Pass.

Without handing him an Honor, you can safely pass Bam7 and Crak5, which you don't need, which don't match anything you've already passed that opponent, and which fall safely within the realm of the types he passed you (Bams, Craks, odds). He passes you Dot7 and Crak9. That's no help, leaving your hand at the following (see **HAND 11.6**).

You're then ready to start the game, and since you're playing as East and have fourteen tiles, you'll begin the game by discarding a tile. You can happily discard Crak9 or Dot7 later, but you may want to discard

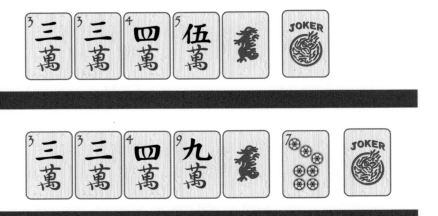

Red Dragon now before someone builds up their hand enough to call it up as a discard.

If you have a good memory, you may notice some tiles you pass in the Charleston coming back to you, such as the Bam7. Conversely, if you pass Winds and you notice that none return, it may mean that someone is aiming for a Dragons and Winds hand. You can also try to recall what you passed to each player to get an idea of what may be in their hand. But for your first games, you shouldn't bother with this. You've just finished a Charleston, so you're ready to begin the flow of the game in earnest.

CHAPTER 12

AMERICAN MAHJONG– STRATEGY DURING THE GAME

Hopefully after the Charleston you're well on your way to a Mahjong hand. If not, you can just spend your first few turns doing the same type of thing you were doing in the Charleston: collecting the tiles that work for at least one of the hands you are looking at in your category, and discarding the tiles that don't. Naturally, the best tiles to get are the ones that are needed by *both* hands you were looking at. But hopefully soon you'll have collected at least nine tiles toward a single hand, at which point you can start focusing on that one.

Reasons to Wait on Melding

Because collecting tiles that you need for your winning hand is your goal, you might be excited if someone discards a tile you need, and want to claim it to make a meld. After all, that will bring you closer to your goal of a winning hand. And indeed, in many cases this will be correct play. However, there are a few things to consider before making a meld:

1. **It passes up a chance to draw from the wall.** Compared to all the other reasons, this is a somewhat minor one, but the fact remains that any time you call up a discard, you're passing up a chance to draw a fresh, unseen tile. If there are tiles multiple players are collecting, you're more likely to get them from the wall than from a discard. And Jokers can't be called up from the discard at all, so the only way to get those valuable Jokers is to draw them off the wall yourself. On

the other hand, if you're calling the discard from the player on your right, you're not really losing out on much wall-draw opportunity, since you're skipping the other players anyway.

2. **It destroys the flexibility of your hand.** This may be the most common mistake for new players, not realizing that by melding a set they are severely cutting down on their future options. This happens in a number of ways:

- Melding locks down the exact number of tiles. Unlike some other Mahjong variants, once you meld a Pung of three tiles in American Mahjong, it is a Pung of three tiles forever. You can't add a tile later to upgrade it to a Kong. So if you're collecting Dot7s and someone discards one, you might call it up to meld it with your pair, but that means your Dot777 Pung is never going to become a Dot7777 Kong or a Quint. New players sometimes lock themselves out of their own hand by not realizing this.

- Melding is a commitment that constricts you to a few hands. Let's say you call a discarded S to meld your Pung of South Winds, eager to complete a Winds and Dragons hand. A few rounds later, you realize that you need a pair of North Winds for the hand, and three Ns have been discarded. Since you can't use Jokers for the pair, you will never get your pair of North Winds. However, with your Pung of South Winds on the table, you are now stuck with that set! The only thing you can do is aim for another winning hand that happens to contain exactly three South Winds. Depending on your scorecard there may not even be another hand at all, or if there is, it probably requires completely different tiles than what you are holding. All the rest of the hands, even if you were close to filling them, are now forbidden to you. Making a meld early in the game can often lead to regret for this reason. Also, even if your meld is a sequence that appears in many hands (e.g., GGGG), melding anything on the table immediately disqualifies you from completing any Concealed Hands.

3. **Melding with a Joker hurts you and helps your opponents.** You can't call up Jokers from the discard, but if you're holding a Crak4 and a Joker, you can call up that first Crak4 an opponent discards to make a Pung of Crak444 with a Joker serving as one of the tiles. And you probably shouldn't, for several reasons:

- First, if a Crak4 is already being discarded and left unclaimed and you have another one in your hand, odds are decent that the other two Crak4 tiles may eventually turn up, whether you draw it or whether it is discarded by your opponents. If you end up drawing more of them, you might be able to make your Crak4 Pung using just natural Crak4s, saving your Jokers for a different Pung that will turn out to be impossible without Jokers because your opponents have melded three of the tiles. Jokers are a valuable resource, and if you use them early, you may not be using them to their fullest potential.

- Second, opponents who draw the tile you used the Joker in place of are allowed to instantly exchange it with the Joker. In other words, when they draw another Crak4 later in the game, rather than discarding it, your opponent may now instantly swap it with the Joker in your Melded Pung, giving you no benefit, but gaining another valuable Joker for themselves.

4. **Last, and perhaps most important: *melding reveals your hand to other players*.** Because American Mahjong uses a score-card that lists exactly what hands use each collection of tiles, melding even a single set can give your opponents a tremendous amount of information. If you meld a Pung of NNN, and that particular set is only used in Wind/Dragon hands, chances are that your opponents may suddenly become stingier with Winds and Dragons. Ideally, you want the first discard you call for a meld to be less obvious if it's early, a set that appears in multiple categories, in order not to give yourself away.

Those are the reasons you might not want to meld too early. Of course, in many cases all of these will be outweighed by the big reason you *do* want to meld: you need that tile to make your winning hand, and there are a limited number in the game! So calling the discards you need is still generally a good thing. Just be aware that there are a few reasons it's not always the right choice—especially early in the game.

Managing Your Discards in the Early Game

Knowing what to pick up may be half the game of Mahjong, but the other half is knowing what to throw away! As always, you obviously want to hold on to tiles for your target hand, and if there's enough overlap with a secondary hand, you may try to hold tiles for that too. But when there are multiple tiles you can discard, there are a few things to keep in mind.

Mahjong is a game that has a flow, and the feel of the game changes from the first few turns to a dozen rounds of the table later. One thing about American Mahjong is that if your table has done both Charlestons and a Courtesy Pass, each player has possibly been handed up to twenty-one tiles in addition to their initial thirteen-tile hand. So it's possible that one of your opponents may be within four tiles of Mahjong before the first tile is even discarded.

Nonetheless, the way you should play in your first few turns is different than later in the game. Even if your opponents are closer than you would like, it is very rare that they will be able to make a Mahjong in the early turns of the game. For this reason, the early game is the time to discard with impunity. If you have a lone Flower you can't use, or random single Honor tiles, throwing it away early lets you get it out of your hand without giving someone else Mahjong. As a bonus, usually you can throw away Honors your opponents need before they have enough copies to call them up from the discard, meaning they have one less chance to get the tile they need.

Early in the game it's important to pay attention to what your opponents are doing, not only with what they might meld but also what they are discarding. Combining these two sources of information might let you figure out what hands they are going for. And it's quite possible that you may have tiles in your hand that they need. Early in the game, if you have a single unwanted tile you think an opponent might need, your best option is probably to discard it, and hope it's too early for them to call it up from the discard.

Unwanted Pairs and Jokers

If you have a pair you don't need, however, your strategy may be a little different. First of all, if you have a pair that doesn't fit your primary hand, but is needed for your secondary hand, hold on to it as long as possible. It may be counterintuitive, but pairs can actually be harder to come by than Pungs.

(You may be asking yourself, "How could it possibly be easier to get three of a kind than two?" Well, there are two parts to that answer. The first part you probably already guessed is discards: you can call up a discard to complete a Pung, but not a pair. And the second half of the answer is Jokers: you can use Jokers for Pungs, but not for pairs. The result is that if you need a pair of Green Dragons, you need to draw two of the four Green Dragons in the game from the wall. But if you need a Pung of Green Dragons, you could draw one from the wall, use a Joker in your hand as the second, and call up someone else's discard for the third.)

So you don't want to discard your pairs if they would benefit you. But even if your pairs are unhelpful for you and possibly useful for your opponent, don't discard them in the first few turns. Midway through the game—and the timing can be difficult to judge, because someone can get Mahjong very fast or very slow; but about nine rounds in—if you have an unwanted pair, you can try to "fish for Jokers."

The way it works is this: you discard one tile from the pair in your hand, hoping that an opponent calls it from the discard to meld an exposure from their hand that includes a Joker. On your next turn, you can exchange the remaining tile from the pair for the Joker in the exposure, which will give you a valuable Joker for your hand. You probably will be able to make good use of a Joker to help finish out your Pungs and Kongs, and on the off chance you find you have no use for a Joker, it will be a safe discard in the endgame.

The trick to fishing for Jokers is timing. If you discard one of your pairs too early in the first few turns, your opponents probably won't be willing, or able, to make the necessary meld with Jokers. And if you discard one of your pairs too late, fifteen turns into the game, you may well be handing your opponent Mahjong! So try to figure out when the game is nearing to a close, and try to fish for Jokers just before that.

Occasionally you'll find that even without any setup, you happen to have a tile in hand that you can exchange for a Joker. Unless you need your tile for a singleton or for a pair, you should always exchange it for a Joker. Jokers increase your hand's flexibility; if you end up not using the Joker it's a safe discard later, and even if you use it for the same tile you exchanged, you've prevented an opponent from potentially claiming the Joker for themselves.

Defensive Discarding Late in the Game

At some point—and again, it's hard to judge exactly when that is, because game length can vary based on many factors; but usually by the time there's about one full wall's worth of tiles left (which will be half of the remaining wall, and then the last half of the starting wall)—it will become apparent that the game is winding down.

By now, at least one player at the table is probably close to Mahjong. Hopefully that includes you! If you're just waiting on one tile for Mahjong, then you can ignore all discarding strategy and just hope to draw your winning tile. If you need two or three tiles for Mahjong, then you can try to improve your hand while still playing somewhat defensively. And if you are more than four tiles away from Mahjong, it's time to accept that you are not going to win this hand, so you may as well throw away winning tiles if that will let you discard more safely.

What Is a Safe Discard?

Mahjong is a game of probabilities, and so once you believe that an opponent could be within one tile of Mahjong, you will want to discard tiles with the lowest possible odds of finishing their hand, lest you end up paying them extra for a victory off your discard. In descending order, here are the safest tiles to discard:

1. **The Joker.** There is only one discard that is always 100 percent safe, and that is the Joker. Jokers cannot be called from the discard pile, and consequently there is zero risk when discarding a Joker that it will benefit an opponent. If, however, you've given up on winning with your hand, that cloud has a silver lining: any Jokers you were going to use to try to win can now be repurposed into 100 percent safe discards.

2. **Tiles outside of winning hands.** In very rare circumstances, all other players will have melded and discarded in such a way as to let you know what hand each player is going for, and so you might be able to identify other safe discards. But absent this rare circumstance, discards are all about playing the odds, and even a strategically well-chosen discard that is safe nine out of ten times means that 10 percent of the time your smart discard will still be called up for a Mahjong. So don't beat yourself up over making a bad discard; it'll all wash out as you play more hands. Nonetheless, it's a good habit to get into: don't only pay attention to what each player has melded, but combine that information with what they've been discarding, and try to figure out what hands they are going for. If nothing else, sometimes you can see an exposure of Bam9999 and check your card to realize no winning hand contains a Kong of 9s and a different color 1.

At that point, you can rest assured that player won't pick up your Dot1 discard—but one of your other two opponents might.

3. **Tiles that have no outstanding matches.** The ideal discard is a tile where the total number in the discard pile and in your hand adds up to 4, meaning that you know for a fact that no other player is holding any of that tile. If you see a pair of Crak5s in the discard pile, and you're holding the other pair of Crak5s, that means there are no more in the game, so your opponents can't possibly have any. Because most of the winning hands require making pairs and Pungs, if you can see that your opponents can't match your tile, it's usually a reasonably safe discard.

- Two caveats to this rule: first, if your opponent is holding a pair of Jokers, they could make a Pung by calling up your single tile. And second, pay attention to hands that only require one of a tile—this will happen most often with Year hands (e.g., 2018) and Winds (NEWS). This is one of the reasons you should get rid of singleton Honors early in the game; it's dangerous to be discarding Winds later on!

4. **Tiles that were recently discarded.** If your opponent just discarded a Green Dragon two turns ago and nobody called it up, you are probably safe to discard it. The more recently a player has discarded a tile, the higher the odds are that it's a safe discard.

5. **Tiles that were discarded a while ago.** These are not as safe as the four previous categories, but still better than the final category of tiles.

6. **Tiles that are completely absent from the discard pile.** Late in the game is *not* the time to discard these. If you've gone through most of the wall and that tile hasn't ever been discarded, that means some copies are hanging out in players' hands, which means they may well be waiting for your discard. The exception to this rule is if you are holding all four copies in your hand and only need three, in which case the tile actually falls under the second category. But otherwise,

if a tile has never been discarded yet, it's quite possible someone will call it up for Mahjong, and you'd rather not be the guinea pig for that little experiment.

Note that special tiles (Flowers, Winds, and so on) are especially bad to discard at the end of the game if there are no copies in the discard pile—and if you are forced to do so, it may be a better option to give up on winning, break up your hand, and discard something safer like a Joker. Of course, if you're only one tile away from Mahjong, you may as well go for it. Sure, you might end up handing someone else the game, but no guts, no glory!

And that's pretty much all you need to know about American Mahjong! The only other thing to mention is the overarching strategy that will help you win more Mahjong games: play more and practice.

MORE ABOUT MAHJONG

While you now know how to play International and American Mahjong, many more variants await the enthusiastic student. The next chapter will discuss some of the many other variants played around the world.

CHAPTER 13

VARIANTS AROUND
THE WORLD

As this book often mentions, Mahjong is the game of a thousand variations. And while the main focus of this book centers on the two major variants of International Rules (played everywhere) and American Mahjong (the most popular in America), there are many other standard variants of Mahjong played all over the world!

Conveniently, if you've already learned the International Rules for Mahjong in Part 2, you will have an excellent basis for seeking out and learning any of the other variants mentioned here. (Meanwhile, American Mahjong is a uniquely American variant, and is dissimilar from any other version of Mahjong played around the world.) If you have learned the International Rules, then you'll be able to understand this list of numerous other Mahjong variants that are played around the world, with brief explanations of how they differ from International Mahjong described in Part 2.

Hong Kong Old Style

This version is similar to International Rules in terms of gameplay, although it uses a Dead Wall consisting of fourteen tiles that can only be drawn to replace Kongs or Flowers. This fourteen-tile wall is separated from the rest of the wall, and is never drawn from to start a player's turn. If the live portion of the wall runs out, the game ends as a Wall Game and is considered a draw.

(As a variant, some tables occasionally play twelve-tile Mahjong where each player is granted an invisible Wild Tile that can be used as any tile. Mahjong is naturally declared much faster and more often.)

The big difference between Hong Kong and International styles is the different scoring methods and payouts. Hong Kong style is favored by gamblers due to the fact that the scoring fans are multiplicative rather than additive, so one fan will double your points, two fans will quadruple your points, three fans will octuple your points, and so on. Historically, this resulted in many gamblers quickly getting in over their heads on the streets of Hong Kong as the numbers could quickly get up to the thousands on a particularly bad hand.

Most modern players mitigate this somewhat by use of expanded fan categories (four, five, or six fans result in a 16-time point multiplication; seven, eight, or nine fans result in a 32-time point multiplication) and a hard maximum limit (ten or more fans caps out your multiplier at 64 times). Thus if you self-draw, it is doubled one final time, meaning each other player pays you a maximum of 128—a large amount to be sure, but still within the bounds of reason, so one unlucky hand won't break you.

Here are the usual scoring fans:

- Pung/Kong of Dragons: 1 point
- Pung/Kong of Seat/Prevailing Wind: 1 point
- Seat Flower/Season: 1 point
- All Flowers/All Seasons: 2 points
- No Flowers or Seasons: 1 point
- All Chow Hand: 1 point
- All Pung Hand: 3 points
- Half Flush: 3 points
- Full Flush: 6 points
- Seven Pairs: 4 points
- Win on self-draw: 1 point

PART 4. MORE ABOUT MAHJONG

- Out on Last Tile of Wall: 1 point
- Out on Last Discard: 1 point
- Out by Robbing a Kong: 1 point
- Out on Supplement Tile: 1 point

There are also a number of "limit hands" that automatically score the maximum amount of points allowed at your table (again, 64 in most modern variants). They are:

- Four Concealed Pungs, win on self-draw
- Three Dragon Pungs
- Three Wind Pungs with Fourth Wind as Pair or Pung
- Four Honor Pungs and Honor Pair
- Four Terminal Pungs and Terminal Pair
- Nine Gates (see International Rules)
- Thirteen Orphans (see International Rules)
- Four Kongs
- Full Flush with a Pung/Kong of Matching Dragon
- Dealt a Mahjong, or call first discard of game for Mahjong

Hong Kong style, with its doubling fan scoring, is the basis for many other variations of Mahjong played around the world. Many other variants use the multiplicative scoring of Hong Kong style rather than the additive style of International Mahjong.

Chinese Classical

Long before the rules of International Mahjong were written out, Chinese Classical rules were fairly popular in China. A few rules differ a bit from the International gameplay, such as the fact that when the dealer wins they deal again (which can sometimes result in a pretty long game if you're waiting for the deal to pass around the full table four times), and that the dealer pays and gets paid double. But the biggest difference with Chinese Classical is this: losing hands can still win points or money.

How does that work? Well, after all players pay the winner, losers pay each other based on the differences in the point values of their hand, calculating whatever points they've managed to assemble. This tends to be a fairly polarizing variant; some players love the idea that you can do reasonably well without being the one to call Mahjong, while other players feel this makes for a duller game. Still, the fact that you can lose the game without losing too much money makes this variant popular with those who enjoy Mahjong as a casual game.

Riichi (Japanese)

Aside from American Mahjong, Japanese Riichi Mahjong is probably the furthest away from the standard rules of International Mahjong. It is also probably the most difficult variant of Mahjong to learn and play well, and is best suited for Mahjong experts rather than casual players.

The bonus tiles of Flowers and Seasons are not used traditionally, but instead a bonus can be claimed through the rare Red 5—a single 5 in each suit (Dot, Bam, Crak) is painted red, and any winning hand that has one of these tiles is worth double the points. A Dead Wall of fourteen tiles is also used, similar to Hong Kong style.

Japanese Mahjong is also much more orderly; there is no large pile of discards in the center of the table. Instead, each player places their own discarded tiles neatly in front of them, so all players may see your history of discards at any time. In addition, any melded sets must have the left, right, or center tile rotated 90 degrees, to indicate which player discarded the tile you called.

Before each hand, a tile is revealed at random from the Dead Wall and the next tile in sequence (next higher number for suits, Winds in seat-play order, Dragons green-red-white) becomes the "Dora" for that hand, doubling the value of any winning hand that uses it. Some players even reveal an additional Dora when making a Kong, or when someone wins off Riichi.

The eponymous "Riichi" (or "Reach") is what you declare when you have a concealed ready hand and need only one tile for Mahjong. You may no longer alter your hand, you are simply waiting for the first winning tile. Declaring this costs you 1,000 points, but if you are the winner of the hand you get an extra Yaku fan. While a fan merely doubles your score, Yaku fans are special in that you need at least one to claim Mahjong (acting like a point-minimum).

The "Hot Tile" Fu-ri-ten rule states that you cannot call a discard to claim Mahjong if you have discarded the tile you are calling earlier in the game.

Scoring is a bit more punishing as well. If the winning tile is a discard, whoever discarded it must pay *triple* the winning score. And East's risks and rewards are doubled: they must pay double if they lose, but gain double if they win.

Note that scoring varies widely depending where you play; Yaku, like All Pungs or Three Concealed Pungs, may be worth only one or two fans depending on your table. Many variants also declare a draw game in various circumstances, such as all players discarding the same Wind on the first round, or all players declaring Riichi, or if there are four Kongs. And a few Japanese variants play with not only Chows, Kongs, and Pungs, but also the Mixed Pung as an optional set—the same number in each of the three suits.

Zung Jung

Fairly new on the Mahjong scene but popular among board gamers, it is no coincidence that Zung Jung was invented by a board gamer: Alan Kwan. Based on the additive scoring of International Rules, Zung Jung uses 44 patterns compared with International Mahjong's 81, but does not have any minimum point requirement to declare Mahjong.

The main differences between Zung Jung and most other variants are the scoring and payout schemes. In Zung Jung, the winner gets no extra points for a self-drawn win; each player simply pays the winner the value of her hand. In the case of a win by discard, players pay equally unless the hand was valued over 25 points. With valuable hands won by discard, the non-discarding players pay 25 points, and the discarding player pays the difference to make the winner's total take thrice her hand's value.

Other Regional Styles

Although the previous variations are the ones most commonly played in America and internationally, there are countless other variations that are popular in specific countries. Here are just some of the many country-specific Mahjong variants played across the globe.

Taiwanese

This regional variation is similar to Hong Kong style, but with a sixteen-tile hand. Players need to get five sets and a pair, rather than four. Kongs are kept completely facedown when declared on the table, and only revealed at the end of the game.

Korean

Korean Mahjong is played without any Bams, so there are only two suits. It is most often played with only three players. Also, you may not call a discard to complete a Chow. Fans accumulate swiftly, like in Hong Kong Mahjong. Some players play with an optional side bet where the first player to reach three Concealed Hand wins gets paid by the other players.

British

In addition to a somewhat different pregame mixing ritual where only South and North mix the tiles, British Mahjong has a few unique in-game quirks. You can only claim Mahjong with a single Chow. There is a mandatory declaration of a Waiting hand, which means when you are one tile away from Mahjong, you must announce it, otherwise you are not eligible to claim Mahjong.

But the most unique rule of British Mahjong is the Goulash: after a draw game in which nobody wins, the game is made easier for everyone by replacing the four Bam2s with Jokers, and then having a three-pass Goulash similar to the American Charleston. Scoring in UK Mahjong is similar to Hong Kong style, using doubling fans with different scoring.

European

While perhaps less popular than most of the variants previously listed, Europe nonetheless has its own collection of Mahjong variants, which differ from country to country.

- **France:** Uses an additive scoring system similar to International Mahjong, but with a different scoring method. France also uses an abundance of special hands.
- **Holland:** Has a special rule for "Bird Eats Cake," which gives you 10 bonus points if your hand's pair is the Bam1 and Dot1, which look like a bird and a cake, respectively. It is otherwise similar to Hong Kong Mahjong, using doubling fans with different scoring.
- **Germany:** The German variation also uses a doubling fan scoring, but has a 100-point minimum to declare Mahjong (usually seven fans, similar to the 8-point minimum in International, but pricier). If you have revealed three melds of a high-scoring Mahjong, anyone who discards the winning tile must pay for the whole table.
- **Italy:** Includes a Japanese Riichi-style mechanic of optionally announcing the Waiting hand for an extra double, as well as an Instant Draw game when all four players discard the same Wind. Scoring is Hong Kong style with doubling fans, including various extras such as the Imbottigliato ("in a bottle") hand, which is four melded sets and winning on a pair.

Mahjong Solitaire

Many people would argue that solitaire isn't even Mahjong, and in some sense, they're right. On the other hand, for many Americans who have never played actual Mahjong and have only played Mahjong Solitaire on their computer, the word "Mahjong" probably conjures up images of this game in their head rather than of the classical Chinese game you've just read a book about.

The rules of Mahjong Solitaire are fairly simple: the tiles of a Mahjong set are arranged in a layered pyramidal structure. Your goal is to remove pairs of matching tiles from the structure until none remain. However, you may only remove "free" tiles, which are not surrounded by tiles on both their left and right, and that do not have another tile resting atop them. If you can remove all seventy-two pairs of tiles from the structure without getting stuck, you win the game.

This game doesn't really have anything in common with Mahjong, but it does use Mahjong tiles, and if you tell people that you are reading a book about Mahjong, at least one person is probably going to think you mean the solitaire game.

FAQ

RULES

Can I pass fewer than three tiles in the Charleston?
Only during the optional Blind Pass, which is the third pass of a Charleston.

What happens if someone passes me a Joker in the Charleston?
Technically speaking, you are supposed to return it, remind them that Jokers cannot be passed in the Charleston, and have them pass you a legal tile instead (not one of the three that they were just passed).

Do I have to match the colors on the American Mahjong scorecard?
No, the number of colors in the hand merely indicates which tiles of the hand must match colors with one another. If a hand indicated 1111 222 3333 444, you could complete it with any two suits, e.g., Dot12 and Crak34, or Crak12 and Bam34, or Dot12 and Bam34, and so on.

Do the suits I'm matching only include numbers, or also the D, F, NEWS?
NEWS refers to the four Winds, and F is Flowers, neither of which have a color, and so they may be used with any suit. D is for Dragons, which *do* have a specific suit—Green Dragon matches Bams, Red Dragon matches Craks, White Dragon matches Dots.

Do I have to match the numbers on the American Mahjong scorecard?
In most cases, yes. When multiple options are allowed (such as the Consecutive Runs section), that will be specifically indicated in parentheses right next to the hand.

Where do you get a zero? I only see 1 through 9.

The Soap Dragon (White Dragon) is used as a zero for the purposes of American Mahjong Year hands. In fact, all Year hands will continue to contain a Soap Dragon until the year 2111.

How do Flowers work?

Depends on what variant you're playing. In American Mahjong, they work like Winds, and can be collected a few of a kind as indicated by your target hand on the scorecard to be used with any suit in completing a hand. In International Mahjong, a Flower drawn is immediately set aside face-up and replaced, and will be worth a bonus point at the end of the game if you win.

Does my Pung/Chow have to have all three tiles be the same suit?

Generally speaking, yes. Some less-common variants allow for Mixed hands, but in both American and International Mahjong, a set specifically contains tiles of the same suit.

Can I hold a Kong in my hand without declaring it?

In American Rules, yes—you may also have Quints or even Sextets. For International Rules, you can hold four of a kind in your hand temporarily to give you options to use the fourth tile elsewhere for a Chow, but a valid Kong must be declared and placed on the table (facedown, if all four tiles were in your hand without calling a discard) so that you may draw a replacement tile. Until you do, you will not have enough tiles to make a valid Mahjong hand that uses the Kong as Kong.

Can you change your mind after you discard?

Technically speaking, once you throw and announce a discard, your turn is over and that tile may only be called by another player, otherwise the next player starts their turn. If it is your first game, however, you may find people willing to cut you some slack.

The player on my left discarded and someone else claimed it. Is it my turn after them?

Nope! If a discard is claimed, the claiming player has usurped the current turn, and play will continue around the table counterclockwise from the claiming player. For this reason, claiming discards from the player on your right can give you an edge over the other two players.

Which tiles do I expose when I complete a set; just the one I picked up, or the whole set?

If you call up a discard to complete a Pung, Chow, Kong, and so on, you expose the completed set. For example, if you call up Bam2 to complete your Pung, you reveal Bam222. If you draw a tile to complete your set, you expose nothing! And of course, if you get your last needed tile and declare Mahjong, then you expose your entire hand.

Can I call up a discard to complete a pair or a Year (i.e., 2018)?

Only if that is the final tile that will allow you to declare Mahjong.

Can I also call up a Joker to complete a pair or a Year (i.e., 2018)?

Double nope! First of all, you can never call up a Joker from the discard under any circumstance. Jokers must be self-drawn. Also, Jokers can never be used for fewer than three of a kind. Patterns like NEWS and 2018 may look like sets of four, but they are actually a collection of four single tiles, and consequently cannot be replaced with Jokers (or called up, except in the case of Mahjong).

Can I exchange for a Joker before my turn, in order to have enough of a kind to call a discard?

Nope! Exchanging for a Joker can only be done during your turn while you have fourteen tiles in hand (that is, after your draw).

What if two people call Mahjong at once, both needing the same discarded tile?

Call priority goes to the player whose turn is soonest after the player who is discarding, to claim the discard for Mahjong. In other words, if the player on your left discards a tile, and you and your right-hand neighbor both call Mahjong on that tile, you would have priority, because your turn was next.

What if one player had just drawn Mahjong, and the other player called Mahjong from the discard?

This one's a little tricky to answer, because it depends on a lot of things. The first answer is, according to the National Mah Jongg League, if a player draws a new tile onto their rack at the same time as another player calls for the discard, the call for the discarded tile takes precedence. On the other hand, this gets into how long your table waits for someone to claim the discard before the window of opportunity closes. Many tables play with a three-second rule, which gives sufficient time for all players to determine whether they need the discarded tile. If the next player waited five seconds and nobody spoke, so she drew a new tile and declared Mahjong only to be interrupted by another player calling Mahjong on the discard, I would say the calling player had missed their chance, and the drawing player has priority. Conversely, if the drawing player only waited a second to draw a new tile and didn't give the calling player sufficient time to see the discard, then the calling player's Mahjong would certainly have priority.

What if two players both have Mahjong in their hands at once, without calling a discard?

Only the active player should ever have fourteen tiles in hand! This is one reason why Picking Ahead is not a recommended house rule. But if this happens, you should probably say that whoever's turn is next is the actual winner, as they would have legally drawn their tile first.

What if Mahjong was called incorrectly?

If it was a mere verbal slip, and the player quickly says, "Oops, never mind," then play can continue. If any tiles have been exposed, then that hand must be declared as a Dead Hand, and the player who incorrectly declared Mahjong is out of the game (but must still pay the winner at the end).

OTHER QUESTIONS

Should I try to win as soon as possible, or aim for a more valuable hand?

Generally speaking, in American and International Mahjong, you're almost always better off taking a sure win than holding out for a more valuable one—and this is doubly true when you're learning. Then again, if you can triple your score with one more lucky draw, fortune favors the bold! (Note: fortune is also extremely fickle.)

Should I always exchange a tile in my hand for a Joker?

Almost always. If you might need that tile for a purpose that isn't three-or-more of a kind (i.e., a lone North Wind tile you might need to use to make NEWS), then you can't use a Joker in a set of singletons or pairs, so you're better off holding on to your own tile. If that isn't the case, however, you should always exchange for a Joker when given the option, for reasons described in the strategy section.

Can I use an American Mahjong set to play International Mahjong?

Sure! Just remove the eight Jokers and you're good to go!

Can I use an International Mahjong set to play American Mahjong?

You'll need to add eight Joker tiles if your set doesn't have them, which might be tricky unless you can find eight extra tiles that look and feel similar enough, so that you can't tell them apart in the shuffle or on the wall. You can then use stickers to convert these eight extra tiles into Jokers.

Where can I buy a Mahjong set?

Many major retailers tend to stock Mahjong sets, so you can check your local Walmart, Target, or any hobby, game, or toy stores near you. There are plenty of Mahjong sets available for purchase online, whether you're buying new sets on Amazon and on specialty Mahjong websites, or used sets on eBay. With used sets, be sure that you are getting a complete set; replacing five tiles can be almost as expensive as an entire set!

Whether you're buying new or used, you'll want to be sure you have the right set for the type of Mahjong you want to play. This means you should pay attention to tile counts—144 is a basic International set (suits, Winds, Dragons, four Flowers, four Seasons), and 152 is a basic American set (International tiles plus eight Jokers). Some sets also include extra blank tiles that can be used to replace lost tiles or for variants.

You'll also want to consider your own preferences in a set—do you prefer the elegance of tiles with Chinese characters and symbols, or do you want sets that also have Arabic numerals in the corners for ease of reading? Do you prefer a set of thinner tiles made to be placed on (included) racks, or do you prefer a set of much thicker tiles that can stand on their own? (Generally speaking, the racks and thin tiles are used for American Mahjong, and the thicker tiles for International Mahjong.)

Where do I get the current year's American Mahjong scorecard?

The NMJL scorecard and rulebook are available for purchase via the NMJL website at NationalMahJonggLeague.org. Various other groups also offer annual scorecards with different combinations (or you can even invent your own!), but as the vast majority of American Mahjong players use the NMJL scorecard, that is the recommended one. While you are learning the game, you may be able to borrow one from a friend, but if you are going to play regularly you will probably want your own.

How do I find a Mahjong game near me?

Ask someone! If you know anyone who plays Mahjong, ask them where they play. If you don't know anyone who plays Mahjong, consider it an opportunity to make some new friends. You might check in at local community centers to see if they know of a regular game. Senior, Jewish, and women's centers are all good places to start looking for American Mahjong, while International Mahjong is more easily found via Chinese community organizations. More broadly, if your town has a community newsletter or bulletin board, you can always see if anyone is posting about Mahjong there, or use it to announce your interest in finding players.

And of course, there's always the Internet. You can find gaming groups through Meetup.com, which is increasingly a useful way to find other folks who enjoy the same recreations as you. You can also do a Google search for "Mahjong" plus "your town name," and see what pops up. You may be surprised how many people play Mahjong right in your town! Also, this book offers a list of Mahjong websites, some of which (like Sloperama.com) have sections to help players find one another. (If you can't find players near you, many of these sites also have links to play online.)

Do I have to play for money?

No, and we wouldn't recommend it while you're learning. International Mahjong is played for points, as China's government frowns on too much gambling. American Mahjong is traditionally played for money, but you could simply stake each player 1,000 points in chips that aren't converted from $10, and just count up point scores at the end of the evening without paying out in cash.

On the other hand, if the tables you want to join always play for money, just try to find one that has low stakes. Some tables use a limit on how much you can lose, so once your chips run out, you continue to play but do not have to pay anyone until you win and regain some chips. If you're playing with a 1,000-point limit, that limits your losses to $10, which isn't too unreasonable for an evening's entertainment.

Do I now know everything there is to know about Mahjong?

No, but you know enough to go out and have fun playing—and that's what's important!

GLOSSARY

Across The opponent sitting opposite from you. Also the middle pass of the Charleston.

Back End The part of the wall counterclockwise from the break point.

Bam Short for *Bamboo*.

Bamboo One of the three main suits. A standard Mahjong set has thirty-six Bam tiles (four copies each of 1 through 9).

Blind Pass An option to pass the tiles being passed to you without looking at them, rather than passing your own tiles. Used on the final pass of the Charleston.

Bonus Tiles The Flowers and Seasons, which are not used to make hands, but are placed to the side when drawn and are worth points when scoring. Note that American Mahjong uses Flowers as standard tiles instead of bonus tiles, and some variants dispense with the bonus tiles completely.

Break The point in the wall where the tiles are separated and dealt from, generally chosen by rolling dice. Also the act of separating the wall.

Calling Claiming a discarded tile for your own hand. If multiple players wish to call the same tile, there is a system for priorities, with highest priority going to the player who is calling to make a Mahjong.

Card See Scorecard.

Characters One of the three main suits. A standard Mahjong set has thirty-six Crak tiles (four copies each of 1 through 9).

Charleston The name given to the series of tile passes that occur before the game starts in American Mahjong.

Chow A run of three consecutive tiles in the same suit (e.g., Crak4, Crak5, Crak6). Also what you call (Chow!) to claim a discarded tile from the player on your left in order to complete a Chow.

Circle See Dot.

Concealed All included tiles are hidden from other players and have not been revealed to call a discard. An entire hand may be concealed, or some sets (such as a Pung) may be concealed while others are exposed.

Courtesy The optional pass at the end of the Charleston.

Crak Short for *Characters*.

Dead Hand If a player attempts to claim Mahjong but has an illegal hand because they have the incorrect number of tiles, their hand becomes a Dead Hand—that player is disqualified and stops playing (although they must still pay the winner), but the Dead Hand remains revealed, to give other players information.

Dead Tiles Any discarded tiles that are not the most recently discarded tile. These tiles may not be called or claimed and hence are called dead.

Dead Wall In some variants, a section of the wall set aside to be used only for replacement draws. When no tiles remain in the live wall, the game is over.

Dealer The player who breaks the wall and deals the tiles. Also known as the East Wind.

Declare Generally to announce that your hand is now a winning hand. Used in other variants to declare Riichi to announce that your hand is one tile away from a winning hand.

Discard The tile from your hand that you place face-up in the middle of the table to end your turn. (Or the act of placing that tile there.)

Dot One of the three main suits. A standard Mahjong set has thirty-six Dot tiles (four copies each of 1 through 9).

Dragon Three colors of Dragon are types of Honor tiles: Red, Green, and White. Four copies of each are in a standard set.

East Wind The first Wind. The dealer is always the East Wind. The East Wind is also the first Prevailing Wind.

Exchange In American Mahjong, the ability to swap a tile from your hand with a Joker in a revealed hand, if you have the tile the Joker is standing in for.

Exposed/Exposure A set that has been revealed face-up to all opponents in order to call a discard. If any set in your hand has been exposed, your hand is no longer concealed. See also Melded Hand.

Fan A collection of sets in a Mahjong hand that are worth a certain number of points. In some variants, such as Hong Kong style, each fan doubles a player's score, while in International Mahjong, each fan has a specific associated point value that is added to calculate the hand's score.

Final Right The third pass of the Second Charleston. Also the last pass.

First Right The first pass of the Charleston.

First Across The second pass of the Charleston.

First Left The third pass of the Charleston.

Flower An illustrated tile outside of the suits and Honors. Not used in some Mahjong variants, used as a standard Pung-able tile in American Mahjong, and used as a bonus tile in many variants (including International Mahjong). Only a single copy of each of the four Flowers is typically in a set, although the four Seasons also count as Flowers.

Hand A winning combination of tiles with which you can declare Mahjong.

Honors Refers to the Winds and Dragons.

Joker A wildcard tile, used mainly in American Mahjong.

Knitted Sequence Tiles three away from one another, meaning 147, 258, or 369.

Kong Four of a kind, meaning four of an identical tile (e.g., four Bam7s). Also what you call to claim a discarded tile to complete such a set.

Mahjong Not only the name of the game, but also the name given to any legal winning hand. The first player to achieve a legal winning hand may declare Mahjong to end the game and claim victory.

Meld A set of tiles that has been completed by claiming a discard, and then placed face-up on the table in front of you. See also Exposed/Exposure.

Melded Hand A fully Exposed Hand composed entirely of sets that have been completed by calling from the discard and are therefore melded onto the table. This hand is worth bonus points in International Mahjong.

Melded Kong A Kong (four of a kind) that is revealed on the table, either because it was formed by claiming a discard or because it was formed by adding to a Revealed Pung (three of a kind).

North Wind One of the four Winds. Sits to the left of East.

Optional Pass After the Charleston is ended, players have an opportunity to exchange a few tiles with the opposite player if and only if both players agree to do so.

Pair Two identical tiles.

Prevailing Wind Indicates the current set of rounds; generally four rounds (one deal for each player) are played under each of the four Winds for a total of sixteen rounds. Some variants also award more points for tiles matching the Prevailing Wind. (And other variants do not use a Prevailing Wind at all.)

Pung Three of a kind, meaning three of an identical tile (e.g., three Bam7s). Also what you call to claim a discarded tile to complete such a set.

Pusher A device made to help move the Mahjong tiles into a tidy wall. These can sometimes be attached to racks.

Quint Five of a kind, meaning five of an identical tile. Note that since there are only four of each tile, this requires the use of at least one Joker tile (e.g., four Bam7s and a Joker).

Rack A small shelf for holding your hand of Mahjong tiles so you can rearrange and look at them all without knocking them over. Generally used in American Mahjong. Can also be used as a verb, meaning to place a tile onto your rack.

Ready Hand A hand needing only one more tile to achieve Mahjong. See Waiting.

Robbing the Kong To claim a tile someone is using to upgrade a Melded Pung into a Kong, as if it were a discard, in order to complete your Mahjong.

Run A set of consecutive tiles in the same suit (e.g., Crak4, Crak5, Crak6).

Scorecard In American Mahjong, the list of valid winning hands and their associated values.

Season An illustrated bonus tile. Only a single copy of each of the four Seasons is typically in a set. (Although they are often considered as additional Flowers for gameplay purposes.)

Seat Wind The Wind matching your current seat (e.g., for the dealer, East).

Second Charleston A second round of three passes, which occurs after the First Charleston only when no player has vetoed it.

Second Left First pass of the Second Charleston.

Self-Drawn A tile drawn from the wall, as opposed to being called from a discard.

Set A set of tiles that legally go together, such as a Chow or Pung.

Sextet Six of a kind, meaning six of an identical tile. Note that since there are only four of each tile, this requires the use of at least two Joker tiles (e.g., three Crak4s and three Jokers).

Simples Refers to the tiles 2 through 8 in the three main suits (Dots, Bams, Craks).

Singles Tiles that stand alone in your hand and are not paired with any like tiles or part of any Chows. Common in American Mahjong in NEWS hands (one of each Wind) and Year hands (e.g., 2018).

Soap Refers specifically to the White Dragon, which is often depicted as a rectangle (or blank) that looks like a bar of soap. Used as a zero in Year hands.

South Wind One of the four Wind tiles. Also is the player on East's right.

Steal During the Charleston, to take a tile from your opponent and pass it to the opponent on your other side as a Blind Pass, replacing one of your own tiles. Also occasionally used to refer to Robbing the Kong.

Suit Tiles Tiles of the three main suits (Dots, Bams, Craks).

Terminals Refers to the tiles 1 or 9 in the three main suits (Dots, Bams, Craks).

Voided Suit A hand that has one of the three main suits (Dots, Bams, Craks) completely absent.

Waiting A player who only needs one more tile to achieve Mahjong. See Ready Hand.

Wall The large stacks of tiles in the center of the table from which the game is dealt and tiles are drawn. Traditionally stacked two tiles high.

Wall Courtesy Refers to the courteous action of using the pusher to push your wall closer to the center when it is being drawn from, in order to make it easier for other players to reach the wall.

Wall Game Term for when players have drawn the entire wall of tiles but nobody manages to claim a Mahjong.

West Wind One of the four Winds. Sits across from East.

Winds Four Honor tiles: East, South, West, and North. Four copies of each are in a standard set. Note that the Winds are also used to determine rounds and dealers in International Mahjong.

Year Hands In American Mahjong, a hand including the current year, such as 2018. The numbers must all be from the same suit (2-1-8), and a Soap is always used in place of a zero.

BIBLIOGRAPHY AND RESOURCE LIST

In writing this book, I read a number of books and websites about Mahjong. If you would like to learn more about Mahjong, you may find some of them worthwhile as well.

Books

Cavallaro, Christina and Anita Luu: *Mah-Jongg: From Shanghai to Miami Beach*

Hammer, Marcia: *Learn to Play Mah Jongg: From Beginner to Winner*

Kohnen, Dieter: *Mah-Jongg: Basic Rules & Strategies*

Pritchard, David: *Teach Yourself Mahjong*

Rep, Jelte: *The Great Mahjong Book: History, Lore, and Play*

Sandberg, Elaine: *Beginner's Guide to American Mah Jongg*

Websites

Sloperama.com: possibly the best resource for Mahjong on the Internet

Museum.Takeshobo.co.jp: International Mahjong strategies from World Mahjong Championship winner Mai Hatsune

MahjongMovie.com

Mahjongg.com

MahJongTime.com

MindMahjong.com

NationalMahJonggLeague.org

WorldMahjong.com

DragonKong.com

INDEX

ABOUT THE AUTHOR

Seth Brown is a lifelong gamer and writer. He has written board-gaming strategy articles and reviews for various sites ranging from *Best Dang Games* to About.com. He has codesigned and playtested various independent games, owns more than three hundred board games, spends an inordinate amount of time on *BoardGameGeek*, and has a local, weekly board-game group.

In the writing world, Seth's award-winning humor column "The Pun Also Rises" has been running for over fifteen years across various newspapers, and currently appears in *The Berkshire Eagle* and *Bennington Banner*. He is a cowriter of two award-winning musicals, is the author of six books, and by the time you read this, will already be working on another book about board games.

His website is RisingPun.com.